We lovingly dedicate this b

Stella & Edgar
2013

My favorite picture of Peggy Lee
It bespeaks of compassion and gentility
-Stella Castellucci

Photo provided courtesy of Stella Castellucci, with permission
from Peggy Lee Associates, LLC

"Harpist Stella Castellucci was standing by – just kind of thinking."

- Marie Mesmer

Daily News Los Angeles

September 4, 1953

"Stella Castellucci accompanies me often which I deem an honor and a pleasure. She is a truly fine musician... and has a quick sense of how the singer would like to interpret the song. All of the improvisation is Stella's... the lovely surf sounds and oriental flavor are particularly nice, I think."

- Peggy Lee

("About the Artists" – ***Sea Shells*** **LP)**

Me in Peg's Dressing Room, Ciro's, Beverly Hills (1955)

Contents

Introduction

Stella Castellucci made an invaluable contribution to many of my grandmother's most iconic recordings, with her elegant harp playing and tremendous musicianship, but more importantly, she was one of my grandmother's dearest friends. How Stella came to be such an accomplished jazz harpist and sought-after studio musician is a fascinating story. Stella has been a part of our family for as long as I have been alive, and I've always known how much my grandmother loved and respected her. In reading Stella's story, I was able to learn about what led her to playing the harp and to working with Peggy Lee, and now I'm even more in awe of her than I was before.

Holly Foster-Wells

Peggy Lee's Granddaughter and Vice President of Peggy Lee Associates, LLC

CHAPTER I

My maternal great-grandparents were Rocco LaTronica and Marianna Minnucci-LaTronica. In the 1880's they emigrated from Italy to Philadelphia. They moved into a row house on Carpenter Street in a poor neighborhood. Their children were: Stella (my grandmother), Carmela "Mary" and Salvatore "Tony."

Stella was one of a pair of twins born in 1889. My great-grandparents were not expecting twins. When the twins arrived, the neighbor ladies went around collecting extra baby clothes for the baby boy, named Jesse. Rocco was a master carpenter. He built one cradle. They placed Jesse in it and they put Stella in an apple box. She proved to be the stronger of the two. She took great pride in telling that story.

The family moved to Los Angeles when Stella was 2 years old. Jesse died at age 13 of influenza. Stella LaTronica and Antonio DeLellis were wed at Saint Joseph Church in Los Angeles on October 5, 1905. Stella was 16 years old and Antonio was 27. This was not an unusual social custom of the time. Antonio was born in Pastina (province of Caserta), near Rome. Antonio had emigrated from Italy to Wales at age 16. He worked there in the coal mines for four years before earning enough money to come to the United States.

Their marriage produced two sons: Dominic Joseph "Don" and Anthony Rocco "Tony" and three daughters: Mariana Virginia DeLellis (my mother), Frances and Carmel. Mama was born on August 5, 1908. They would later adopt Agnes "Aggie" Bellomo after my Great-Aunt Mary's death.

Antonio became successful in real estate. His affluent position allowed him to give his children a privileged lifestyle. Mama came from a disciplined and sheltered upbringing. The children took great care to not abuse their privilege. They were expected to practice great respect for their elders.

Engagement Day of Antonio DeLellis & Stella LaTronica (1905)
Top Row: Rocco LaTronica (Great-Grandfather)
Row 2: Salvatore "Tony" LaTronica (Great-Uncle) & Carmela "Mary"
LaTronica (Great-Aunt)
Row 3: Marianna Minnucci-LaTronica (Great-Grandmother), Antonio
DeLellis (Grandfather) &
Stella LaTronica (Grandmother)

Saint Frances Xavier Cabrini was born in Lombardy, Italy in 1850. She came to the family's backyard in East Los Angeles when Mama was a small girl. She remembered it well and told us about it. Mother Cabrini was just starting an orphanage and school called Villa Cabrini Academy in Burbank, California. She was interested in buying an oil press from my Grandfather. She needed it to make olive oil in the kitchen of her orphanage. My Grandfather would not sell it to her but gave it to her as a gift. Mama recalled this tiny nun patting her on the head as she walked away. How could they know that they were looking at a future Saint?

Mother Cabrini died in Chicago on December 22, 1917. She was canonized by Pope Pius XII on July 7, 1946. I well remember that day. It was publicized all over the world. She was the first American citizen to be canonized. Her picture is framed over the entrance to my kitchen where I can see her every day.

Mama attended the private girls' high school, Saint Mary's Academy. When she was a freshman her parents gave her a new Buick "Roadster." It had a convertible top. I have seen pictures of her standing in front of it with Uncle Don and Aunt Frances. They were all good-looking young people.

Uncle Don in Military School

Uncle Don was Mama's younger brother. He was born on October 12, 1909. He passed the bar at Southwestern University School of Law in Los Angeles. His classmate and childhood friend was found to have cheated on the exams. Uncle Don out of loyalty would not confirm the truth against him. He and his friend were therefore disbarred.

Thereafter Uncle Don took over and bought a small grocery store in East Los Angeles. It had previously been owned by Vincent Bellomo, Aunt Aggie's father. We all called him Uncle Jimmy. I was fond of him as a small child. Uncle Don and Aunt Nettie were good to me. They had three children: Don Jr., Mary Ann and Mark. They lost a newborn baby girl named Joanne Marie between the first and last two children. Uncle Don died of a heart attack in January of 1958. Aunt Nettie survived him many years.

Uncle Tony was Mama's youngest brother. He was a running back for Loyola University at Los Angeles. He would serve in the US Army during the WWII years. After that he became head coach at his alma mater. His wife, Aunt Norma was special in our lives. Like Aunt Nettie, Uncle Don's wife, she was extraordinarily kind and loving. It was as if they had been blood aunts to us. Uncle Tony and Aunt Norma lost a newborn baby, their son, Timothy Richard. He was born after their other two children, Tony Jr. and Karen.

My father Louis (Luigi) Stanislaus Castellucci was born on October 26, 1897 to Teresa Porcelli and Giovanni Castellucci. Daddy was born in Apice, Province of Benevento, Italy. The name Apice comes from the fact that this tiny ancient hill town is on the Appian Way. The Appian Way was an important road in ancient times.

Grandmother Teresa trained as a midwife in Naples. She never came to the United States. I did not get to meet her before her death in 1953. Grandfather Giovanni and his three brothers were symphonic bandmasters in Italy. Daddy was the only one of his father's six children to follow him into music. Daddy learned to play trombone as a boy from the town bandmaster. He played in the bands of several small Italian towns as a boy and teenager.

Daddy and his father emigrated from Naples and arrived at Boston Harbor in 1912. Like most teenagers, he was always hungry. The moment they disembarked his father took him to the nearest little café. The waitress brought them a menu. My Grandfather unknowingly pointed to something. They did not know any English at all. When she returned they were given two plates of apple pie. This was their first taste of American food. Apple remained Daddy's favorite pie for the rest of his life.

As a teenager in Staten Island, New York, Daddy played in his Uncle Omero's Italian Puglia Band. Daddy and my Grandfather lived with him. In his late teens and early twenties Daddy toured the United States with the John Phillip Sousa Band. He was virtuosic on the Eb cornet and baritone horn. He played operatic arias that were traditionally sung. The band accompanied him, as would an operatic orchestra accompanying a singer. My Grandfather conducted the American Navy Band and taught for four years before returning to his family in Italy. Daddy never saw his father again and his father died in 1936.

Chautauqua was a wonderful humanitarian organization. Daddy toured their circuit as part of Castellucci's Neapolitans. His Uncle Omero Castellucci was conductor. Omero composed *The Prince of Peace*, a successful three act opera. It was based on the life of Jesus. It was composed in the Italian lyric style. He was educated at the International School in Rome. The great composer Pietro Mascagni was director there. Omero appeared before the King of Italy, Victor Emmanuel at the Quirinale Roma by royal command.

Daddy apprenticed under his Uncle for conducting band music while living in Staten Island. Castellucci's Neapolitans consisted of: Catherine (Omero's wife) on trumpet, lyric soprano Edna Howland, Daddy on violin and guitar and my Great-Uncle Pindaro Castellucci (Omero's brother) as the euphonium soloist. After playing in the Neapolitans, Daddy played in Castellucci's Concert Band. Daddy was 19 years old when he began conducting the Castellucci bands.

William Jennings Bryan was a statesman from Nebraska in the late 1800's and 1900's. He was a popular speaker of that time. The Castellucci band accompanied Mr. Bryan on the Chautauqua circuit. They traveled to entertain the troops. Daddy played the brass instruments. Mr. Bryan chose him as his "secretary." When Daddy was not playing in the band, he would wait in the wings before Mr. Bryan came on stage to give his lectures. When Mr. Bryan was ready Daddy would come out to hand him a glass of water. That was the extent of his secretarial duties.

Here are some assorted press quotes that give some detail on Great-Uncle Omero's various bands that toured the Chautauqua circuit:

"Castellucci's Italians, a musical concert company of seven men, playing twenty-five different instruments are giving the program this afternoon. The opening number was 'The Chautauqua March,' composed by Mr. Castellucci himself. Then came the 'Misere' from *Il Trovatore*, 'The Last Rose of Summer' and 'Tipperary.'"

Daddy (1920's)

"Omero Castellucci, the peerless bandmaster and the royal entertainer of the multitudes is coming with his Boston Marine Band of select artists for a Big Musical Festival Day at the Chautauqua. It will be the great holiday and gala occasion of the season."

"There's a bracing exhilaration – a riot of feeling – passes through one when the [Royal Blue Hussars] band begins to play. One hears the tramp, tramp, tramp of marching feet going steadily down to battle, as the brasses flare their call to arms and the drum beats out its everlasting step, step, step. The baton is in the hand of Louis Castellucci. His greatness lies chiefly in the wonderful effects he has achieved by the patient training of the talented group of musicians under his skilled direction. The band is brilliantly costumed in the dashing blue of the Hussars. Its playing is brilliant. That every member of the organization is a musician of the first water is proved by the many special features produced as solos and special instrumental groupings including such novelties as a string quartette, a xylophone trio and an ocarina sextet. In addition, further zest and variety is added to the program by Miss Eva Quintard, grand opera star."

"Chautauqua week brings splendid music of every kind in abundance – from the stirring airs of Castellucci's Concert Band to the rare orchestral music of the Zedeler Symphonic Quintet. Omero Castellucci, famous band director brings to Chautauqua on the fourth day his great organization of Italian Musicians. For several years they have been the feature of Eastern Chautaquas. First Western Tour. One of the best bands in the West this year."

"Castellucci and his musicians and Miss [Bess Gearhart] Morrison arrived here this morning and the announcement was made that an exceptionally fine program will be given the patrons of the Woodland Chautauqua."

Sometime later, Daddy came to Los Angeles looking for work. Soon he was playing in the Vitaphone Studio orchestra. They could be heard in Warner Brothers feature films. They played for silent films including those of comedian Harold Lloyd. Daddy was also conductor of his Venice of America Band and Santa Monica Municipal Band. He became a member of the Los Angeles Philharmonic from its beginning in the 1920's with Otto Klemperer as conductor.

One day, Daddy saw a picture of Mama at the home of mutual friends. He wanted to meet her. They had one date that was chaperoned by Uncle Don and Aunt Frances. Mama had never been on a date before she met Daddy. She was 21 years old and unworldly. Daddy was 32 years old and a "man of the world," so to speak. My parents married three months later on November 27, 1929. They wed at Saint Cecilia's Catholic Church. They shared about the same age difference as my grandparents. My parents moved into their first home together at 4279 Walton Ave. It was in Los Angeles and across from Mama's parents' home. It was also near Saint Cecilia's.

Wedding Day of Louis & Mariana DeLellis Castellucci
(November 27, 1929)

Daddy was a studio orchestra player from the late 1920's. He played bass trombone, his main instrument. He went on to work for Warner Brothers, MGM (Metro-Goldwyn-Mayer), Paramount, 20th Century-Fox and Universal. He was in the recording orchestra for the first talkie, *The Jazz Singer* (with Al Jolson, 1927). He was what was termed as "first call" bass trombone in the studios. He would play on the early Shirley Temple films and the Fred Astaire & Ginger Rogers musicals at RKO Studios in the 1930's.

Some of the scores Daddy played on were: Max Steiner's *Gone With The Wind* (1939), Franz Waxman's *Rebecca* (1940), Leopold Stokowski's *Fantasia* (1940), Walter Schumann's *Night of The Hunter* (1955) and Dimitri Tiomkin's *Friendly Persuasion* (1956). In addition to radio and television shows, he worked for film composers: Alfred Newman, Bronisław Kaper, Constantin Bakaleinikov, Victor Young and Miklos Rosza. He played in the orchestra for the original NBC (National Broadcasting Company) radio series *Dragnet* and its subsequent television series.

CHAPTER II

I was born Stella Castellucci on October 14, 1930. I was named after my maternal grandmother, Stella LaTronica-DeLellis. I was christened as a baby at Saint Cecilia's Church in Los Angeles.

Saint Cecilia was a musician in the early days of the Christian faith. She married a nobleman named Valerian whom she converted to Christianity. She, her husband and his brother Tiburtius were martyred during the reign of the Roman Emperor Marcus Aurelius between 161 and 192 AD. Saint Cecilia is known as the patron saint of musicians.

I am grateful that my parents were married in Saint Cecilia's Church. That was their parish and that of my grandparents. It was an interesting coincidence, considering my future life in music. Saint Cecilia's was the elementary school where my younger sister Luanna, my brother Louie and I attended. Her picture was prominently displayed at Saint Cecilia's School.

"Tuppie" is the nickname I have lived with all of my life. I am used to it. I have been called that by my entire family and extended family. Only at school and with friends am I called Stella. It came from my Grandmother. She spoke perfect American English with no trace of an accent. She would play with me, throwing me up and down in the air. She would try to say "Betty Boop" and "Tuppie" is what came out. *Betty Boop* was a cartoon character that appeared in newspapers and films. She made her debut the same year I was born.

One of my earliest memories is walking around and seeing cracks in the cement of our backyard. This was after the Long Beach Earthquake in March of 1933. It was devastating and killed many people.

Uncle Don's store was across the street from one of Los Angeles' first daycare centers. Mother Cabrini Day Home was located at 1406 Mateo Street. I was sent there before kindergarten and grade school. The nuns kept me until Uncle Don could close his store late in the afternoon and drive me home. I remember the good Sisters there.

Their Order was founded by Mother Frances Xavier Cabrini. It is called the Missionary Sisters of the Sacred Heart. Mama and her younger siblings were taught Catechism there. They were raised in that East Los Angeles neighborhood. Their nun teacher was Sister Giovannina. I remember her well. She kept in contact with Mama throughout her life. I sent all of Sister's letters, Christmas cards, Easter cards, handmade holy cards and other items to the Order in New York for their archives.

My sister Luanna Maria Castellucci was born on June 19, 1934. Luanna and I got along well as small children. Before she was born, I was yearning for a sibling to play with. Mama instilled the ideals of her childhood lifestyle in Luanna and me. This continued throughout our young adult years and even later. Mama was loving and supportive of what we chose to do with our lives.

Daddy was not so much a disciplinarian, but he had his moments. He was emotional and possessed a temper to which Mama was not accustomed. That temper was, however, canceled out by a sweet side. He possessed a liberal attitude toward life in general. He had a gentle and sympathetic side, especially in a family crisis. Daddy didn't want to teach us Italian in order to improve his English.

Daddy loved to be with his musician friends. Mama entertained them often at home with home-cooked dinners. Luanna and I loved being around Daddy's friends and their wives. We grew up seeing most of them often. One of Daddy's hobbies was to have barbeques. He passed this tradition on to us.

Daddy composed a civic march entitled "Let's Go to Santa Monica" in 1934. This song was dedicated to the city he loved so much.

Victor Schertzinger conducted many memorable film scores on which Daddy played. He was also a movie director. Daddy not only played in the orchestra for his film *One Night of Love*, but appeared in a brief scene. The scene was with its star, Grace Moore. She was an American international opera singer. The film won the Academy Award for Original Score in 1934. Grace Moore was killed in a plane crash in 1947. Daddy said she was so kind and nice to him on the set.

I have a third cousin on Daddy's side in The Bronx, New York. She is a Dominican nun stuck with the same nickname "Tuppie." Her name is Stella, after her mother. She is now known as Sister Theresa Angelo Girolamo. We are always in contact. When we sign our letters and cards she signs "Tuppie N.Y." and I sign mine "Tuppie L.A." The poor thing took the nickname as naturally all of her life as I did. She must be about 70 years old now. She is active in charity work in her Dominican order.

Tuppie N.Y.'s father was Ralph Girolamo, Daddy's first cousin. Ralph's mother was Amelia Porcelli, a sister of Daddy's mother, Teresa Porcelli-Castellucci. Aunt Amelia and her sister, Lucy emigrated from Italy to New York. They married and had children. Lucy's son was Pete Porcelli.

When Pete and Ralph were young men they came to Los Angeles by car to visit Daddy. They were houseguests of my Grandmother. Her home was much larger than my parents' and it was just across a large yard. My Grandfather Antonio DeLellis built it. He died in 1932 in a car accident caused by a stroke.

Somehow Ralph and I bonded. He would take me for rides in his and Pete's Model T Ford when he was running errands for my Grandmother. She never drove in her life. She had a Packard bought by my Grandfather. It was long with two folding extra seats in the back. Luanna and I loved to sit in it and pretend we were in a limousine. The car was so big to us.

One day, on a ride with Ralph, I was misbehaving while he was driving. In desperation he said "Tuppie, if you don't behave I'm going to make you get out of the car and walk home!" He did make me get out and I belligerently started walking. He then slowly followed me at a distance. This was the origin of how he started closing his letters and cards to me. He would draw a car with tracks of a little girl walking away from it. He would write the caption: "Out!!" When I would write to him I closed my letters the same way. He died on April 2, 1992 of Lou Gehrig's disease.

Aunt Aggie was born on June 30, 1921 in Los Angeles. Her mother, my Great-Aunt Mary died of complications from childbirth. She was only 24 years old. We called her Aunt Mary as if we had known her. We became familiar after hearing so much about her. She was divorced from Aunt Aggie's father Vincent. Aunt Aggie was raised from the age of 2 as their own by my grandparents Stella and Antonio DeLellis. She lived like a little princess among their five other children who loved her so much. She was sent to Saint Mary's Academy, the same private girls' high school as Mama, Aunt Carmel and Aunt Frances.

With her being across the yard, Aunt Aggie and I were in close contact every day. She was only 9 years older than me. She became my Godmother at that early age. My Uncle Don, who was 22 years old, was my Godfather. Aunt Aggie would take me to weekend matinees at our local movie theatre. This cemented my memories of all those wonderful songs from the musicals.

More importantly, Aunt Aggie took what was then called "popular piano" every week. This began when I was 5 years old. I would sit in a corner of my Grandmother's living room while she took her lessons. I took in all those wonderful songs from the Great American Songbook. She is totally responsible for that. I would hear her play the songs of: Jerome Kern, Rodgers & Hart, Harold Arlen, Irving Berlin, Gershwin, Cole Porter and so many others. This went on for three years. She played well and sang the lyrics sometimes.

I was so fascinated with the music. Aunt Aggie had loads of sheet music to all those songs. Many of the covers had pictures of movie stars who made films that featured some of the songs. When Aunt Aggie died in 1995, her sweet daughter Marianna sent me a box. It contained all of the sheet music. I treasure it. Looking at those covers brings back so many happy memories. Tommy Dorsey is on the cover of "I'll Never Smile Again." "High on A Windy Hill" is another beautiful song you don't hear much anymore. There is a pink cover of Ginger Rogers and Fred Astaire dancing to "The Carioca" and "Cheek to Cheek." Peg recorded a version of "Cheek to Cheek" as well as many others among the sheet music.

Aunt Aggie loved jazz music and she passed that on to me. I heard her play "Lookie, Lookie, Here Comes Cookie." It had to be my first time hearing jazz. I also heard it on the radio. It was written by Mack Gordon and recorded by Cleo Brown. It was a popular song released in 1935.

Me & Luanna (1935)

Many years later, "Lookie, Lookie, Here Comes Cookie" came up during a conversation with Peg and Ed Kelly. He was her wonderful and kind road manager. We called him Kelly. I told them my funny little story about it. Being the imaginative typical small child, I would create visions of my own. I used to stand on the sidewalk outside of our home. I would look way down the street as far as I could. I was hoping to wait and see "Cookie" come down my street. Peg and Kelly laughed so much they couldn't stop. I had no idea "Cookie" was a man. That name made me picture a girl. My distant cousin, Dan Mattrocce, is now over 90 years old. He lives in San Francisco. From early childhood he was nicknamed "Cookie." I think he must have been given that name before the song came out.

When I was in kindergarten, our class would paint watercolors with little aprons on. We would have a milk and graham cracker break. That time was interrupted when I got chickenpox and was not brought back. My teacher Miss Olivia Baker was so nice to me.

In 1st grade at Saint Cecilia's School, I was not able to complete a class craft project. We were supposed to use white material, cotton for stuffing and buttons for eyes to make a cat. I could not sew it up. I cried so hard I was bawled out by Sister Francis.

I would cry when the school nurse came. She visited at intervals to give us free shots for one disease or another. Richard Green always seemed to be standing in line near or behind me. He would try to console me. He was just as scared as I was. This was done in the school library. No one was ever allowed to visit it or to borrow books by order of Father Brady. He was pastor of Saint Cecilia's Church and School. He was a good priest, but so strict.

Father Brady was old and walked with a cane. One could not walk on his treasured lawn, especially not dogs. You got caned if you did. He did not really hurt us; he just tapped us on the legs. However, he had a sense of humor and was not overly unkind if not pleased with report cards. He came once a month to read them in every classroom. One Christmas play at Saint Cecilia's glistened with magic. The older student actors were memorable.

Daddy wrote "La Serenata de La Fiesta." It was the official song of the Fiesta de Los Angeles (or 150th Birthday celebration) in September of 1931. The lyrics were written by Charles N. Felder. Daddy had been conducting his own bands each summer in Santa Barbara, California. This was for the annual "Fiesta Days."

Santa Barbara is a historic Spanish settlement. It goes back to the early days of California. The mission there was founded by Father Junípero Serra.

Daddy's band played well-attended concerts. They were given each Sunday during the two-week celebration and at other times. When Luanna and I were 2 and 5 years old we attended one. Luanna was attached to Daddy. One Sunday, she got up from where we were all sitting. In the middle of a piece the band was playing, she walked up to the bandstand and yelled "I want my Daddy!" He had to stop conducting. Much to her protesting, he picked her up and brought her back to where we were.

Luanna at Daddy's Band's Concert (1936) - "I want my Daddy!"

Leonard Torres was a classmate from 1st through 8th grades. His brother, Ralph, was Luanna's classmate. We see the brothers and their wives, Rose and Marie occasionally.

My 2nd grade classmate Eddie McManus appeared in the Shirley Temple film *The Littlest Rebel* (1935). Shirley Temple was my idol as a child. He was in a birthday party scene with a speaking line. He was dressed in a small boy's formal suit of the Civil War era. I was so proud of him when I saw it. He had told me about it. He lived close to me. We often walked to school together. I never saw him again after 8th grade graduation. I often wonder what happened to him.

Another sweet childhood friend was Patricia "Pat" Whaling. She was a classmate all throughout grammar school. She lived on our block and was my constant playmate. She got married after graduating from Our Lady of Loretto High School. Then we lost contact.

For the Christmas of 1937, I had received a two-wheeler bike. I promptly rode it during Christmas vacation every day until returning to school. It was a cold winter. I rode fast. Because of this combination of sweating and cold air getting into my lungs I contracted pneumonia.

On the first day of school in January, I became ill. I walked home the few blocks. My Great-Grandmother Marianna Minnucci-LaTronica saw me through her breakfast room window. She lived with my Grandmother and her family. Luanna and I were surrounded by this wonderful big family.

My Great-Grandmother intercepted me and brought me inside. She knew that Mama and my Grandmother were out shopping. She observed that I had a burning fever. She covered me on the living room couch. She waited until Mama returned to have her call Dr. Hanlon, our family doctor. She never learned how to use a telephone.

I was not expected to live, antibiotics didn't exist yet. Pat was sent by Sister Alice Cecilia, my 2nd grade teacher, with a gift. She brought me a little plaque of the Blessed Virgin Mary. This still stands in my bedroom. Dr. Hanlon ordered a serum he deemed would be the only recourse that might save me. It had to be flown from New York in a biplane. That took three days because of the bad weather. It did save my life.

When I recovered from pneumonia, my Great-Grandmother was the first person I was taken to visit. After being bedridden for many weeks, I could finally walk again unaided. This joyful reunion stands out ever-so vividly in my memory. She was always making bread. I would hide under the kitchen table where she was kneading the dough. I thought she couldn't see my hand pulling off a piece of raw dough.

Me & Luanna with Uncle Tony DeLellis (1938)

In May of 1938 at Saint Cecilia's Church I made my First Communion at age 7. This was four months after recovering from pneumonia.

My Great-Grandmother died that same year. She died in her bedroom at my Grandmother's home. I vividly remember seeing Mrs. Stager. She was our ever-present neighbor in family emergencies. She was kneeling and praying just outside of the room. This was my second experience of loss in our family. My Great-Grandfather died in 1936. Being in a funeral home both times was unreal for Luanna and me.

Daddy, Mama, Luanna & Me (1939)

Aunt Carmel wed David Hall in 1939. She was the younger of Mama's two sisters. Luanna and I were flowers girls at her wedding. She and Uncle David had eight children: David Jr., Anthony, Michael, Christopher, Christine, Patrick, Rocky and Dennis.

Mama insisted that Luanna and I walk home from school for lunch. Once home, we would listen to disc jockey Al Jarvis' *Make Believe Ballroom* on the radio. He played the current popular music and jazz. We were sometimes late returning to class.

From the age of 9 I began to stutter. It got to the point wherein I was terrified to be called upon to recite or read aloud in class.

Luanna and I were 5 and 9 years old when we had our pet

goat, Rochester. We named him after Jack Benny's butler played by Eddie Anderson. This was on Benny's radio show *The Jack Benny Program*. Our Rochester was a beautiful white kid. We would feed him his milk from a baby bottle. Before Easter Rochester went missing from our Grandmother's garage. We were told that he must have run away. We grieved terribly.

The holiday dinners were always at our Grandmother's home throughout childhood. When Easter Sunday came we sat at the dinner table. Luanna and I looked at each other and at the huge tray of cooked meat. We knew it was Rochester. We sat there and did not eat anything for dinner. We were under the impression that he was a pet for us to keep. We didn't know that he was intended for the dinner table for Easter. It was an unintentionally thoughtless thing to do. Otherwise we were cherished by our family. They all knew what we were thinking and so the day went. We left the table and didn't speak to anyone for the rest of the day.

CHAPTER III

I am the only one of Daddy's children to follow in his footsteps. I loved music from the beginning of my life. I began piano lessons with Daddy at pre-school age. I continued for a few years with Mrs. Dora Nizamis, Aunt Aggie's piano teacher. After that I had lessons with Miss Lenore Metzger, the organist at Saint Cecilia's Church.

Daddy said I had a "fine touch" at the instrument. I felt intimidated by the black keys, going only so far as the keys of: C, F, Bb, Eb, G and D. Daddy had been teaching me solfège (ear training). This is the application of the sol-fa syllables to a musical scale or to a melody. He also taught me theory and harmony. These disciplines helped me identify and learn the chord changes of the Great American Songbook.

I wanted to be like Aunt Aggie. I struggled with piano until I stopped when I was 10 years old. I often went to symphonic concerts with Daddy. We shared a deep musical bond. That is where I got my first sight of a harp. It was played by May Hogan-Cambern. She and Daddy were on stage playing in the Los Angeles Symphony conducted by Werner Janssen. This was at the Wilshire Ebell Theatre.

The beauty, size and sound of the harp fascinated me. I immediately asked Daddy if I could try to learn to play it. He let me start harp lessons when I was 11 years old. I found the harp much easier to get around. I had a smaller version of the large concert grand harps. I am grateful for this harp that started it all. I still have it and it is now over 100 years old. Daddy bought it secondhand. It is a Washburn style #14. It was built in 1914 at the Lyon & Healy harp factory in Chicago. I do not know who the previous owner was. It was not being used for commercial work. It is perfectly suitable and useful.

I subsequently had nine years of study with four teachers of classical harp literature. I loved these experiences. They have remained with me. They are useful in my approach to the playing of: jazz, popular music, the Great American Songbook and all of those wonderful song composers of the 20th century.

Nowadays children are starting at a much younger age and doing well. This is due largely to the invention of folk harps. These are much smaller harps suitable for small children. They are portable and less expensive. There is also the cláirseach or Irish harp, a small harp that stands on a table. This is a much older version of the folk harp.

Lucia Laraia worked with Daddy in the early days of sound movies in the 1920's and 30's. She was an excellent harpist. She recommended her niece Aïda Mulieri-Dagort as my first teacher. Daddy was then conductor of his Los Angeles County Band. This band included harpists Aïda and May Hogan-Cambern. *The Catalina Islander* had this to say about Daddy: "His natural sense of perfect pitch, musical virtuosity and artistic interpretation affords him qualities responsible for the exceedingly fine performances of the band." I have a picture of Aïda with Daddy's band.

Aïda worked with her aunt at Warner Brothers. Aïda was an excellent harpist. They played on film scores when there were two harps in the orchestra. She was on contract at Paramount for many years. I only knew Aïda as my first teacher for two years. She was quietly spirited, gentle, educated and a fashionable dresser. She was so patient with me.

My lessons started with a most wonderful method book by Charles Oberthür. It was entitled *Universal Method for The Harp*. He was a 19th century European harpist. He achieved considerable fame as a teacher and harp virtuoso. His book is still published for use. It contained many musical studies in a progressive sequence of style and difficulty. There were exercises for every technique. It was excellent training in playing and musicality for which I am ever so grateful. Aïda started me off with an excellent foundation.

Maxine Longmuir was a classmate. Her mother invited me to

Maxine's birthday dinner. I felt so special to have been invited. It was only her parents and a family friend, a young woman named Marcella.

Paul Mauro was a first cousin of Uncle Sam. Paul taught me how to play Ping-Pong at my Grandmother's home. I asked him and his wife, Lena to be my Godparents for my Confirmation.

I was confirmed at age 12 at Saint Cecilia's Church. I took my paternal Grandmother's name, Teresa, for Confirmation. Uncle Sam and Aunt Frances often took me to visit them in Long Beach, a short distance from Los Angeles. I loved going to see them. They were so loving to me and fun to be around.

Dorothy Evans joined our class in the midterm of 6th grade. She came from Utah. Her stuttering was as bad as mine. She was brave enough to read aloud and was not laughed at. We used to commiserate about our affliction. She told me about her desire to become a nun. She lived across the street from me. When I began 7th grade Dorothy had transferred to another school.

When I was in 8th grade, Sister Agnes had everyone recite a paragraph from a school health magazine. When my turn came, one of the sentences I read aloud started with an "m." It felt like an eternity before the word "many" came out of my mouth. The class started to laugh. I was so embarrassed that I ran out of the room. Sister found me in the hall crying hysterically. She called Mama to take me home. It is still painful to recall.

Catherine Ketsdever sat directly behind me. After this incident, she would automatically stand up and take my place when I was called upon. This was at my request and with permission from Sister. Catherine was a real friend to me. Claire Gerhard sat across the aisle from me. She must have felt sympathy for me in my stuttering. She always called me "Dear." She once told me that I was "fragile."

Joseph Quintile was my second harp teacher. Daddy sent me to him for lessons. Mr. Quintile was born in Italy. His wife Marian was a studio harpist. He lived in the United States in the 1930's, 40's and 50's. He returned to Italy in 1959 with his second wife and young daughter. My lessons were not for a long period because he became busy at MGM Studios.

Mr. Quintile was an extraordinary harp virtuoso. He preferred to work in the commercial field of music. He was most interested in motion picture studio recording. I once heard him play *Introduction and Allegro*, a concert piece for harp composed by Maurice Ravel. It was originally composed for harp accompanied by a small chamber group. Mr. Quintile played all of the accompanying orchestral parts together with the harp part. His arrangement was unbelievably stunning, especially for a 14 year old.

My early lessons were somewhat fragmented by the effects of WWII. These years were exceedingly hard for our family, as they were for everyone else, single or raising a family. We lived on rationing coupons. These were used for food, shoes and gas. Meat was limited so there were "Meatless Tuesdays" to save it for the troops. Cooking and bacon grease were saved in cans and delivered to the food markets. This collection was for the war effort for use in the defense industry. Everyone was growing a "Victory Garden" in their backyard for vegetables and fruits. We were busy with that as children.

Daddy was conductor of the Los Angeles County Symphonic Band. I would attend their concerts in Pershing Square in downtown Los Angeles. They helped to sell war bonds. Their concerts were broadcast on NBC Radio weekly. The band was accompanied by John Raitt. He was a handsome young man with a beautiful baritone voice. His daughter, musician Bonnie Raitt, was born in 1949. One of my favorite songs from that time was the Nat King Cole Trio's "Straighten Up and Fly Right."

Aunt Aggie wed Harry Earl "Bud" McEntarffer in Lincoln, Nebraska on August 15, 1942. This was shortly before he was shipped out overseas during WWII. Uncle Bud was born and raised in Lincoln. He entered the army on December 23, 1940. He served in France and Germany during WWII as a Technical Sergeant with the 134th Infantry Division. While he was away their son Harry Earl Jr. was born in 1943. Aunt Aggie worked in the Douglas Aircraft factories.

Aunt Aggie & Uncle Bud

Uncle Bud was permanently injured in combat in the European theater and was discharged on March 1, 1946. He received the Purple Heart and Silver Cross for his service. He had to use a brace for his leg because of the shrapnel. Uncle Bud taught Luanna to make her bed as the army requires. The sheets have to be pulled so tight that one can drop a dime on the bed and it bounces off. She insisted on making her bed like that. She would not allow anyone, including me, to sit on it.

I had Uncle Bud honored in the book *Home of the Brave (Profiles of American Veterans)*. I submitted his words for it: "It was the flashback and nightmares from the years of remembering the day we lost our outfit during a shelling and lost almost all our men. Those brave young men we had to leave behind as I crawled for help with my Captain on my back. It was in Nancy, France. We had not even a chance to learn their names when the shelling started. Being new to it they clustered instead of scattering. I put tourniquets on the Captain's legs and we got out of the area having to leave them behind. The worst was not being able to stay in the service. 100% disability would not let me back in. I tried, I would have done it all again."

Their daughter Marianna was born in 1946. She was named after my maternal Great-Grandmother Marianna Minnucci-LaTronica. Harry Jr., Marianna, their children and grandchildren still live in Lincoln. I call them on Aunt Aggie's birthday. Marianna lived with her husband, Larry Dvorak, a retired policeman, until his death on January 16, 2013.

CHAPTER IV

I graduated from 8th grade at Saint Cecilia's in June of 1944. I was not allowed to go to a Catholic girls' high school. This was a mandate strictly enforced by my Grandmother. No one in my family could argue with or persuade her as much as they tried. She thought I was already too quiet and shy and would end up becoming a nun. My Grandmother said it would be alright for Luanna but not for me.

I didn't even have a vocation to become a nun but Luanna did on her own. She was constantly asked if she would like to enter the convent by her teachers. This persisted even later at Mount Saint Mary's College. That is where she earned her Bachelor of Arts degree in education. She would have become a nun except that Mama was not happy with the idea. I cried and begged that whole summer to no avail.

On July 6, 1944 my baby brother Louis "Louie" Stanislaus Castellucci was born. I remember the first time he came home. He had a sweet face, blue eyes, fair skin and dark brown hair. He was "Castellucci-looking" and resembled Daddy. Luanna and I helped take care of him. We would take turns rocking him to sleep, preparing formula for his glass baby bottles and changing his cloth diapers. We used a purple ointment for his diaper rashes. There were no plastic baby bottles or disposable diapers then. We played with him as though he were a precious doll.

John Audubon Junior High School is where I went for 9th grade. This was my first experience in a public school. In the middle of the school year, Father Schnieders called my parents. He had been my Catechism teacher in 8th grade. He was organizing a student talent show at Saint Cecilia's. He remembered that I was studying harp. He asked if I could play a harp solo for the program. He suggested I wear a long dress. I didn't have one of my own.

Aunt Norma gave me one of her formals to keep. It fit perfectly. We added a bit of fine net at the neckline. It was the same color as the formal.

Mr. Quintile sent me to Maryjane Mayhew Barton to continue my lessons. I called her Miss Barton. She had been a former pupil of my final teacher, Mr. Alfred Kastner. He told me that she was an exceedingly fine pupil and player. She went to Philadelphia to study with Carlos Salzedo, famous for his *Modern Study of The Harp*. He founded the harp department at The Curtis Institute of Music. Mr. Kastner expressed his disappointment at her defection to Philadelphia.

Miss Barton became one of Salzedo's many disciples. His "modern method" included a radical change in hand position while playing. He wrote a great body of compositions for harp. Miss Barton didn't impose that change of hand position on me, nor did I ever see her use it herself when playing. For this I am ever grateful. I was by then used to the relaxed hand position I had been taught by Aïda Mulieri-Dagort.

"Largo" is from Handel's opera *Xerxes*. It is originally an aria for a tenor. Miss Barton selected and coached me in it. The music was arranged by Salzedo. I played it for the talent show at Saint Cecilia's. This was my first experience playing in public.

Miss Barton would come to our home for my lessons. She gave me almost exclusively the Salzedo music to study, especially his book *Five Modern Etudes*. They were, for me, technically difficult but interesting. Some were beautiful in a modern sense, removed from the classical idiom. In that one year I never got through the entire five etudes. I learned an integral and important aspect of harp playing. That is tuning the instrument properly. For that I am grateful to Miss Barton. She was an unusually sweet person and patient with me.

Luanna and I later visited Miss Barton in Santa Barbara, California. She lived the remainder of her life there. Aïda and Maryjane had different teaching styles. They both expected excellence and exercised enormous common sense.

I accompanied the boys' and girls' glee clubs for the Christmas program at Audubon. Mrs. Hartshorn was their conductor. I was their only accompaniment. This was another first for me. I played as they sang "O Holy Night (Cantique de Noël)."

Audubon's orchestra was my first experience in playing harp in an orchestra. Daddy brought my little harp there every time a harp was required in the orchestra's repertoire. Miss Dorothy Matson was our conductor. She was a professional cellist. The first harp part I played was from Edward MacDowell's suite for orchestra *Woodland Sketches*. The selection was entitled "To a Wild Rose."

I graduated from Audubon in June of 1945. Aunt Norma gave me a powder blue suit to wear. It was made of lightweight wool.

I began 10th grade at Manual Arts High School. It was two blocks away from home. Manual Arts was called that because they specialized in the arts. They had curriculum for: painting, woodworking, printing, ceramics and sculpting. Fortunately, the music department was exceptional.

Manual Arts was famous for its former students: war hero General James Harold "Jimmy" Doolittle, Metropolitan Opera tenor Lawrence Tibbett and actress/singer Kathryn Grayson. Miss Grayson lived across the street from us, farther up the block. She lived there for many years before us until her death in 2010. She was friendly and sociable.

I took Spanish as an elective in junior high school and 10th grade. I didn't need to use it for any reason but I loved it. I had a choice of two electives in addition to my music studies: typing or home nursing. I was afraid that with typing I would be a terrible pupil. I thought I would fail. I failed algebra twice in junior high, so I took home nursing. I learned how to change a bed with a patient in it and did well.

In September of 1945 I was referred by May Hogan-Cambern to study with Alfred Kastner. She was one of his early pupils in Los Angeles. May suggested to Daddy that I was ready for more serious and sustained studies. Daddy agreed to the idea. Mr. Kastner was 75 years old. He was Viennese and Victorian in personality. He always wore a suit and tie. He was of the "Italian School" that used a relaxed hand position. This was taught to him by Antonio Zamara, his teacher at the Vienna Conservatory.

I inhabited a supremely beautiful old world every Saturday afternoon. My lessons usually lasted two hours. At the end of my lessons, Mr. Kastner's daughter Stephanie would appear rolling a cart. She would serve us fragrant English tea with cookies. Mr. Kastner was gentle, even if my slowness or lack of understanding sometimes tried his patience. He expected excellence. He made me want to work hard and I wanted him to be pleased. I began practicing seriously and diligently.

Mr. Kastner taught me an appreciation of the great master composers. This remains in my memory with great love. He gave me an introduction to the classic harp literature of the Romantic era. This included Hasselman's *Petite Valse* and piano transcriptions from the works of: Mendelssohn, Mozart, Liszt, Saint-Saëns, Beethoven, Bach's *2-part Inventions* and orchestral parts from Wagner's operas. There were also pieces by: Tournier, de la Presle, Samuel-Rousseau, Pierné, Galeotti and Loukine. Mr. Kastner had an enormous library of harp music.

While teaching me Debussy's *Danses Sacrée et Profane*, Mr. Kastner told me that he played them in London with Debussy conducting and Maud Allan dancing. The *Danses* were originally intended to be danced to. While teaching me the cadenza from *The Nutcracker Suite,* he told me that he played it with Tchaikovsky conducting.

Mr. Kastner's living room walls and piano held several framed photographs. They were inscribed by famous musicians and composers he knew and worked with. These included: Fritz Kreisler, Claude Debussy, Maurice Ravel, Sir Edward Elgar, Sir Thomas Beecham, Gustav Mahler, Camille Saint-Saëns, Sir Henry Wood, Arnold Bax and Jean Sibelius.

I met Ann Mason-Stockton in 1945 at Mr. Kastner's home. He had a forthcoming engagement as first harpist with the Orquesta

Sinfónica Nacional in Mexico City. This was for a period of six months. He asked Ann to come and meet me. He wanted her to give me lessons in his absence. Ann was delightful.

Ann was born on October 30, 1916 in Santa Barbara, California. She lived with her mother and older brother, Thomas. Her parents divorced when Ann was a small girl. When they moved to Los Angeles their next door neighbor was a young girl studying harp. Ann was fascinated by the instrument and Mrs. Mason asked Ann to take it up. Mrs. Mason found or was referred to Mr. Kastner. Ann started her lessons with him at age 9. Mr. Kastner told me that Ann was his "premiere pupil." She was presented in recital at age 11. When she was 14 years old, she won the Theodore Presser Scholarship to the National Music Camp in Interlochen, Michigan.

Ann majored in English and music at University of California, Los Angeles (UCLA) in the 1930's. She took Arnold Schoenberg's class in music composition. He taught there for many years. There is a concert hall on the campus named for him. He was born in Vienna in 1874 and died in 1951 in Los Angeles. He was one of many great European composers, musicians and artists who fled the Nazi regime. Ann graduated with a bachelor's degree.

Ann became second harpist for the Los Angeles Philharmonic from 1936-1941. Mr. Kastner was first harpist. She was living in Hollywood with her husband, Stuart. She was an inspirational teacher, much like Mr. Kastner. I loved hearing her play the music she had assigned me to study. Only many, many years later did I learn from her that I was the only harp student she ever accepted. She taught me because of Mr. Kastner's request. She was a busy studio player for films and radio and had no desire to teach. She drove to our home for my lessons after school.

Louie often appeared at the sliding glass door of the practice room/library. It was located just off the living room. He would stand there to watch me practicing. He was fascinated by the harp. I sometimes took him inside. I would place him on the side of the bottom base of the harp (support column). He was so small he was able to stand on it. When not being held between the right shoulder and two knees for playing, the harp could rock if held securely. I would rock him a little as with a rocking chair. He loved it, especially if I sang a nursery rhyme or little song he knew. Ann took great pleasure in seeing Louie's fascination.

My first professional job was in 1946. I had just become a member of Musicians' Union Local 47 in Los Angeles. I was now eligible to play on a professional recording. It was for Daddy's album of military band music entitled *Here Comes the Band*. He conducted his Los Angeles County Band. He was on contract with Capitol Records for heading the concert band department. This was not nepotism. Daddy merely decided I was ready for a professional recording job.

The band received fine critical reviews and Capitol was happy with them. I was nervous and scared but did a professional job. It helped a lot having had a year of orchestral playing at Manual Arts. That was comparable to a college course in a large music department. Around this time I played a concert at the Hollywood Bowl. I was part of a symphony orchestra of student musicians conducted by Leopold Stokowski. I played on Daddy's second album entitled *A Festival of Symphonic Band Music* in 1950. Daddy composed "Stand By March," one of his most popular marches. It was later used in the Cecil B. DeMille film *The Greatest Show on Earth* (1952).

Tawny was a golden purebred cocker spaniel puppy. She was given that name by her previous owner, a musician friend of Daddy's. Louie was 2 years old when he got his first pet. He loved Tawny so much. He thought it would be alright to drink from Tawny's water bowl. After the initial shock everyone howled with laughter. He thought teasing her was part of playing with her. One time she had finally taken enough and bit Louie on his bare back. It was summer time. He was only wearing his little play shorts. The resulting scar was a keloid type; it left a pronounced puffiness of tissue. He carried this reminder of Tawny for the rest of his life.

My "Sweet Sixteen" birthday party took place on October 12, 1946. My uncles, aunts, young cousins ("baby boomers"), parents, Luanna and Louie were there. Three classmates attended, all of whom I had met at Audubon Junior High School. We were all at Manual Arts by then. They were: Lucille Caso, Gloria Gravley and Marie Gomoll. They were secretly invited by Mama and were a great surprise. Aunt Aggie and Uncle Bud were still living in Los Angeles before moving to Lincoln, Nebraska with their two children.

I had been ill that year with an advanced case of anemia. I had lost a lot of weight. I had a pretty navy blue crêpe dress. Mama bought it for me some time earlier. She suggested I wear this dress to show some of my aunts who hadn't seen it. New clothes were a rare occurrence in our immediate family. No one was what was then called "comfortable." I put on the dress and it fit me fine.

Everyone always entered Grandmother's home through the big kitchen's back entrance. It was a matter of habit. I knew the family was getting together that Sunday as usual for dinner. I didn't know a party was going to happen. When my parents, Luanna, Louie and I came into the living room, everyone yelled "Happy Birthday!" I started to cry immediately like a baby. There must have been a wonderful dinner buffet and cake, knowing the way the women went about things like that.

I was given a box full of little engraved calling cards. Graduating students would use them to give to their classmates, which for me would have been the summer of 1948. I received a lovely bracelet with scroll work from an aunt. I received a sterling silver letter opener with an engraved "S" from an uncle. My Grandmother gave me her engagement ring from 1905. The gold on the ring was scrolled with a small raised diamond in the middle. I wore it rarely because I was afraid I might lose it. I later showed it to Peg and asked her to try it on. Her hands made it look as beautiful as it was. I would give anything to relive that birthday party with all of the family intact along with my school friends.

I played a concert for the Easter of 1947. I was part of a group of high school musicians. Mama went with me to Salt Lake City with this orchestra. We played at the historic Mormon Temple.

My one and only solo recital included *Première Etude de concert*, Mr. Kastner's composition for harp. This was at Mr. Kastner's home in the summer of 1947. Ann Mason-Stockton attended. Early in the day, she had thoughtfully ordered an orchid corsage. It was delivered to Mr. Kastner's home for me to wear on my dress. It was the first time I'd seen a pale green orchid. This dried flower remains a treasured keepsake.

Mr. Kastner took me through Ravel's *Introduction and Allegro*. I found it more difficult than Debussy's *Danses Sacrée et Profane*. Mr. Kastner suggested I play *Danses Sacrée et Profane* at Manual Arts' annual spring concert. I played it with the string section of the school orchestra. I was tearfully overwhelmed when he and Stephanie sent flowers to the concert.

I was a junior in high school when I met Kathryn Julyé-Gilbert. She and Daddy played in the NBC orchestra for the weekly broadcasts of Sigmund Romberg's show. He was the composer of several operettas performed on Broadway and in films from the 1920's, 30's and 40's. Daddy would take me with him to meet Kathryn. I watched her rehearse and play the actual broadcasts. It was summer time and I was out of school. She invited me to sit next to her during rehearsals. I was fascinated at her expertise. I found her to be warm and welcoming. She came from San Francisco and was a fine singer as well.

Composer Victor Schertzinger's daughter Paula and I were friends since I was a teenager. She was a wonderful harpist. Her husband, Stanley Chaloupka was first harpist with the Los Angeles Philharmonic. Paula was second harpist with him. Their conductor was Alfred Wallenstein. They were with Daddy in that orchestra since its resurgence in 1943. They were both in their 20's when they got engaged.

When Louie was a small boy, he was brought to the Saturday morning children's radio broadcasts. Daddy would take him to listen in the concert hall. I was always with them. Louie's first sight of Stanley at the harp gave him the idea that Stanley was his guardian angel. Louie considered him so and that delighted Stanley. Paula did not play for the children's concerts. They only used one harp for the broadcasts.

I had a memorable experience when my parents and I were invited to their engagement party in 1948. I was requested by their daughter, Kamila, to write of that experience at Stanley's funeral service in 2002. The story appeared in *Overture,* the official monthly publication of Musicians' Union Local 47. Stanley lost Paula one year before during a trip to Sydney, Australia. They came to our home when Daddy was alive and many times thereafter. Stanley came once or twice after Paula died. He grieved so much he did not live long after losing her.

Mr. Kastner died in May of 1948. This was one month before I graduated from high school. I was his last pupil. I studied with him for three years. His harp music library was given to me by Stephanie Kastner. Knowing his Victorian personality and preferences, I pray he understands and pardons my defection to jazz and popular music. I credit my ability in these realms to my foundation in classical music theory and harmony.

To Dear Stella,
His lovely and gifted pupil.
In remembrance
A Kastner
May 23, 1947

I was a major in music at Manual Arts for three years. I was a member of the junior and senior orchestras. Our conductor was

Mr. John Farrar. Many years later I played for his funeral at the request of his family. Some of my courses included: Chorale (taught by Mrs. Harriet Laidlaw), Harmony [I, II and III] and Counterpoint (taught by the wonderful Miss Lenore Snow), fine art (taught by Mr. Swankowsky) and English and American Literature (taught by Miss Edna Joy Addison).

The school had a fine football team. The huge stadium was named Wilson Field, after a former and beloved coach. I yearned for the experience of going to Saint Mary's Academy, where Mama, three aunts and Luanna went. I was miserable most of the time, but it turned out to be a blessing in disguise. This was because of the quality and great diversity of Manual Arts' music department. The study of composition, theory and arranging was also in their curricular. I do keep and cherish Manual Arts in my heart and memory.

My High School Graduation (1948)

In 2009 I received an email from Tom Street's son. Tom was an orchestra classmate at Manual Arts. He played trumpet. His son found me through a harp website. Tom and his wife were living in Loomis, California, a suburb of San Francisco. Tom wanted to reconnect with me after all those years.

My harp was stored in a small closet in the orchestra room between daily classes. Tom had volunteered to move it for me. He carried it from the orchestra room to various locations on campus. His sister, Lily May Street played French horn in the orchestra. It was a bolt out of the blue to see Tom and his sweet wife, Anna. They visited our home several times for lunch and dinner when in town. This continued until Tom's death in 2012.

When I learned that Patricia "Pat" Whaling from Saint Cecilia's School had died, it was particularly hurtful news. In July 2013, I learned of Lucille Caso-Switzer's death from her daughter. She was one of my friends who attended my 16th birthday party. I attended her husband's memorial service in 2009 in Fallbrook, California.

June Fernand-Landsberg was in the school orchestras of Audubon Junior High and Manual Arts with me. June taught violin in Texas' public schools. Her husband, Phil Landsberg was a professional trumpeter who died in 2013. Joan Connelly-Irving died on March 27, 2013. She was in my civics class at Manual Arts. Hearing of the death of a classmate has always brought its own special feeling of sadness and reality.

CHAPTER V

After I graduated high school, I stayed home for a year. I declined attending college due to my fear of public speaking. I did not know that one is not expected to stand up and recite or speak in front of the class. My stuttering mercifully and gradually began to disappear. After a while no one seemed to notice it.

I was "freelancing" as it is called. I was working odd jobs in local orchestras for one-time events. Johnny Johnston was a popular singer and was married to Kathryn Grayson. He had a two-week engagement at Ciro's the fall after graduation. Ciro's was a posh nightclub on the Sunset Strip of Beverly Hills. Sonny Burke was the conductor and there was a house band. Someone in the union must have booked me. It was my first time in a nightclub. I didn't enjoy it and felt uncomfortable. There were two shows nightly. I did see a lot of movie stars. Rosalind Russell and Loretta Young attended with their husbands. Everyone had to be dressed up to be in Ciro's. Ladies wore long formals and the men wore tuxedos.

On May 11, 1949 I played a concert with baritone John Lambardi and the Bay Cities Symphonic Band. This was at the Long Beach Municipal Auditorium to raise funds for the orphans of Italy. I also played as part of the Dorothy Wade String Trio at the Los Angeles County Museum of Art (LACMA) around that time.

I played for 1 ½ years in Ted Bacon's Golden Strings. This was a professional all-female string ensemble of fifteen musicians. I was the youngest member of the group. We played at various events and concerts. Special arrangements were made for us by Mr. Bacon. This was a fine experience in ensemble playing and required a lot of responsibility. Ann Mason-Stockton played in the ensemble at the beginning of her career. Another Kastner pupil, Elizabeth Ershoff-Hamburger had been a member as well.

Kathryn Julyé-Gilbert called Daddy telling him to have me audition for the ABC (American Broadcasting Company) Radio Orchestra in Hollywood. She was too busy at NBC. There was a quota law wherein you could do only so many broadcasts per week. The auditions were to replace her. I was wary since studio work required sight reading and minimal rehearsal. I gave it a try and got the job after my audition. I started on my 19th birthday, October 14, 1949. I was making $97.10 per week, which seemed like a fortune to me. I was scared to death of the microphone standing next to the harp.

Work began at 1:00 PM. All music was played by the staff orchestra. We did six radio broadcasts each week, including two musical shows and two live television shows. Our conductor was Basil "Buzz" Adlam. He composed cue music and wrote most of the musical variety arrangements. Friday broadcasts featured one of the members playing, accompanied by the orchestra. Harp was one of the featured members. The network had my name shortened to Stella Castle for broadcasting. ABC did not consult me. I remained Stella Castle for all of the orchestra's musical broadcasts.

The Sunday afternoon musical show featured popular singer Richard Hayes. Another of the weekly musical shows featured the popular singer, Polly Bergen. She later became a fine actress in movies.

I played on several dramatic radio shows at ABC. One of them was *A Date with Judy* with Richard Crenna. He was young and played Judy's boyfriend. Many of the radio actors would go on to act in television and film such as: Hans Conried, Virginia Gregg, Gerald Mohr and Elvia Allman. One of the shows was directed by Blake Edwards. He was not yet married to Julie Andrews. Another program I played on was *Meet Corliss Archer*.

One particularly special live broadcast featured: Ethel Barrymore, Judy Garland and Anne Baxter. Judy Garland was friendly and sweet to me. I could hardly talk to her. The way she looked at me made me feel she knew what it was like being so shy. Another special we did featured: Bing Crosby, Dinah Shore and Buddy Clark. Buddy Clark was an excellent and popular singer who was killed soon after in a plane crash. One of the television shows we did was a variety show featuring well-known people.

This was around the first time I saw Peg. I was a fan of hers. I had the Mañana single (released *1/5/48)* and her album Rendezvous *with Peggy Lee* (released 3/29/48). She had her own radio show down the street at CBS (Columbia Broadcasting System). Walter "Pete" Candoli was in the orchestra for Peg's show. Pete was also in the staff orchestra at ABC while I was there.

I was on a long break from a show at ABC. I went to visit my friend and mentor, Ann Mason-Stockton. Ann was playing harp in the orchestra, conducted by Sonny Burke. Ann had taken over my harp lessons after our mutual teacher Alfred Kastner's death. I didn't meet Peg that day. Being shy, I just stayed in the empty audience seats until Ann was finished. When they took their break I visited her.

Louie was a big fan of *Hopalong Cassidy*, a cowboy series on television, as well as other westerns. He would pretend to be a cowboy, complete with his cowboy boots, hat and holster. He would be running as if on a horse after the "bad guys." He even sang his own background music. All of this took place on the sidewalk facing our backyard. Anyone walking or driving by could see him. Luanna and I would watch from where he couldn't see us.

I was introduced to my first boyfriend by Aunt Carmel and Uncle David. The gentleman was a doctor and first cousin of Uncle David. I was a month short of being 20 years old and he was going on 29. He was a pathologist interning at a major Catholic hospital in Los Angeles. For someone as sensitive and emotional as he was, it amazed me that he selected this specialization. He took his medical degree from Creighton University, a Catholic school run by Jesuit priests in Omaha, Nebraska. He was an only child, born in Hollywood. He was educated in Catholic elementary and high schools there.

In the spring of 1951 he was inducted into the Air Force during the Korean War as First Lieutenant. He was being sent to Alaska. He would head the department of his specialization at the Air Force Hospital. Shortly before he was sent out his father died suddenly. We had already broken up. That was my choice because

I was not in love with him. I didn't really know what it was to be in love, as he was. I didn't even know how to appreciate having someone in love with me.

The relationship was formal, in keeping with my strict upbringing. His dear mother was sweet and fond of me. After her husband's funeral she hugged Louie. He was then going on 7 years old. He was so responsive to her. This image stays with me and brings me to tears. As a child Louie was a bookworm. He usually had a storybook under his arm. He was in 2nd grade at Saint Cecilia's.

The Silver Anniversary for the National Conference of Christians and Jews was held in November of 1950. The theme was "Brotherhood Through Music." Concerts were held at the Cathedral of Saint Sophia in Los Angeles. Louis Stanton was the originator and producer. I played with harpists: Maryjane Mayhew Barton, Louise Clow, Cheryll Scott-Butterman and Nancy McDonald-Youngman. We were accompanied by violinists: Jacob Heiderich, Mildred Hill, Roland Hill and Kathleen Risch. Together we were known as The Hollywood Harp and String Ensemble. The ensemble was led by Maryjane Mayhew Barton.

In 1951 I quit my job at ABC. I decided to explore my career as a harpist and began to freelance again. These experiences led to session and film work. I was just one month short of my 21st birthday when I played on my first film scoring session. I played in the orchestra for Charlie Chaplin's *Limelight*. This was the real starting point for me in the recording industry. Claire Bloom, the co-star of the film sat in the studio close to the orchestra. Her character's name was Thereza. She was knitting the whole time.

Mr. Chaplin supervised every aspect of the film including directing and starring in it. He got his way but did it without being arrogant. He attended every scoring session. I was seated at the harp just five feet away from Mr. Chaplin, who was at the podium. I was scared to death. I was clearly in his view. I was nervous when the red light turned on in the studio to begin recording. I thought he would find something in my part to complain about but he didn't.

Mr. Chaplin conducted only the main title. He made many comments to the orchestra regarding how he wanted it to be interpreted. He talked at great length in specific terms. He was knowledgeable and even coached the players. He wrote the music for "The Terry Theme." I was surprised by his musical abilities and handling of the orchestra. Perhaps someone harmonized the chords under his melody.

The rest of the score was conducted by Keith Williams. It was arranged by Raymond Rasch and Russell "Russ" Garcia. I went to see the film for the first time in 1972. It was revived at an art movie theater in Beverly Hills. The film won the Academy Award for Original Dramatic Score. I believe *The Great Dictator* (1940) is Chaplin's work of genius. His "Hitler" speech and acrobatics in that film are extraordinary. Jack Oakie made a perfect "Mussolini."

Luanna and I were ardent fans of *I Love Lucy*, especially when it started in 1951. During the Lent season of 1952 we gave up watching it every Monday night. It was pure agony. Nancy McDonald-Youngman was the harpist in Ricky Ricardo's (Desi Arnaz) band. She had been a pupil of Maryjane Mayhew Barton. Miss Barton would tell me of her abilities. I got to know Nancy briefly before she died. She was a sweet, regular person in her relationships to colleagues and friends. Her accomplishments are truly impressive.

Daddy brought me to a special one-time broadcast at NBC on February 24, 1952. World-renowned concert violinist Jascha Heifetz was guest soloist. Ann Mason-Stockton and Daddy were in the orchestra. Ann was pregnant with her son, David. She was playing in her maternity suit. It is my everlasting and loving memory of David. My family and I knew him as a sweet and cordial child and young man. He took an interest in taking up the harp for a short time as a small child. Ann named him for the biblical King David, who played the harp and slew the giant Goliath.

Louie's first dog Tawny died shortly before we moved to our second home in January of 1953. It was located at 3867 Mount Vernon Drive in Los Angeles.

Aunt Frances and Uncle Sam Sarracino had three children: Frances Ann, Ross Paul and Rocco. We called Uncle Sam the "joy-maker." Aunt Frances and Uncle Sam invited me along with their friend Peggy and her husband to Las Vegas. We went to The Sands to see Frank Sinatra. He was in his prime at the newly-opened Copa Room. There was dinner before the show. Sinatra sang with an orchestra. I was thrilled to see him on stage. I also saw his great pianist Bill Miller. Bill remained Sinatra's pianist until Sinatra's death. Afterward, we went to the Thunderbird and Last Frontier hotels.

Another score I played on was for Robert D. Webb's film *Beneath the 12-Mile Reef* (1953). The score was composed by Bernard Herrmann, best known for his work with Alfred Hitchcock. The other harpists in the orchestra included: Maryjane Mayhew Barton, Helen Bliss Hutchison, Cheryll Scott-Butterman, May Hogan-Cambern, Zhay Clark Moor, Paula Schertzinger Chaloupka, Louise Steiner (wife of Max Steiner) and Ann Mason-Stockton. This stands out as I knew almost all of these women personally. It was only my second film scoring session.

I was studying with Antonio Cafarella. He was an old friend of Daddy's. He was an arranger for Daddy's symphonic band. I am so grateful to Daddy for sending me to this kind and gentle old man. As a young man he was flutist with the orchestra of the Academy of Saint Cecilia in Rome.

Cesare De Sanctis authored a book on pure four-part choral writing entitled *La Polifonia Nell'arte Moderna*. Mr. Cafarella studied this particular method with De Sanctis until emigrating to the Unites States. This was in the late 1800's or early 1900's. It is still used today. This solid foundation is totally responsible for the way I voice a jazz chord. I often use my training in the study of harmony and four-part choral writing (soprano, alto, tenor and bass). It was an exhausting and rigid course of study. I kept with it twice a week for four years.

I corresponded with my first boyfriend after he was sent to Alaska. This lasted 2 ½ years until I stopped answering his letters. I had not accepted his proposal of marriage after three months of dating. I didn't have anyone else in my life, either.

Me (April 5, 1953)

In April of 1953 I received an invitation by mail to his wedding on May 2nd. I was very quiet and unhappy as I was dealing with it. He and his wife became fine family friends. We entertained them in our home and they did the same for us. I played at his funeral, at the request of his wife and children.

I wanted a home with a husband and children but was not ready. I grew up sheltered in an old-fashioned Italian family. I lived at home with family as always. I went to work when the work came, which was not regularly. I would get an occasional orchestra job or recording session.

One day in June of 1953, I had just come home from what would be my final lesson with Mr. Cafarella. I received a phone call from Pete Candoli. He was a well-known jazz trumpeter, and a member of Peg's group. We had worked together in the staff orchestra at ABC. I hadn't seen him since leaving ABC. The conversation went something like this:

Pete: *Stella... I'm at Peggy Lee's house. We are rehearsing with her group for an upcoming tour. We are beginning our engagement* *at Ciro's in one week. Peggy has always loved harp and wants to add it to the quartet. Come on over, bring your harp and sit in!*

Me: *Pete, I just don't think I'm the person you want. How could I do that? I've never played jazz or with jazz musicians!*

Pete: *I know how you play. I used to listen to you playing alone backstage on broadcast breaks. You would be "noodling" (jazz term for improvising) around on the tunes. I know you can do it. You know the tunes and you've got ears, so come on over and give it a try!*

(After much protesting, he finally won.)

Me: *Alright, I will give it a try.*

Pete then gave me directions to Peg's home in Holmby Hills. I was simply astounded. I had never met Peg nor given a thought to playing in a jazz group. The words "harp" and "Peggy Lee" didn't seem to go together. Peg admired the sounds of a harp. She had a recording of New York harpist Laura Newell playing Ravel's *Introduction and Allegro*.

While at ABC, I liked to sit and run through tunes in different ways. I didn't know Pete had been listening or ever noticed. I wasn't even driving yet so I asked Daddy to take me. He loaded my Lyon & Healy style #22 in our station wagon and off we went. Daddy was excited for me.

We arrived while they were in rehearsal that afternoon. The door opened and we were greeted by Lillie Mae Hendrick. She was Peg's cook and housekeeper. She said "Come right in! Miss Lee is expecting you. They are all in the living room rehearsing."

Peg came up to me and extended a strong handshake. She said "Hi Stella, I'm Peggy. Won't you sit down with us and listen for a while? When you feel like joining in, just jump in when you feel like it." I listened to them go over their material and "hung my ear out," as we say in jazz. You're not reading music, you're making music. The group consisted of: Pete Candoli on trumpet, Martin "Marty" Paich on piano, Joe Mondragon on bass and Frank Capp on drums. Today, Frank Capp leads the renowned jazz orchestra

Juggernaut.

Well, that's what happened. They were in the middle of Cole Porter's "I've Got You Under My Skin." I knew that song well. It was cemented in my memory. Somewhere around the bridge (transitional passage connecting two sections of a song) I went to the harp and began chording around. We were "faking" as the term goes, without music. Playing in a jazz group is "faking" of the highest order. And yet, perhaps "faking" is a convenient but erroneous term.

What the musician actually is doing is creating: the endless colors of harmony with substitute and altered chords, the rhythmic surprises of anticipation or suspension, the constant improvising on and away from the melody and the give and take of rubato playing. All are the subtle elements of jazz. We played jazz and the great songs I grew up loving and knowing. I went through a few more songs with them. We went on for about an hour before Peg called a break. She said nothing to me regarding the rehearsal. I had no idea what Peg would be like. I just knew that I liked her right away.

We all had a wonderful dinner prepared by Lillie Mae. Peg had graciously invited Daddy to join. After dinner we were all having coffee and dessert. I noticed Peg standing in a corner of the living room. She had exquisite taste. She had a beautiful ram's head chair. It would remain in all of her subsequent homes. She was making her way around talking to the musicians. I had a feeling they were discussing me as they occasionally looked at me.

I didn't think I would make it. I felt I had bombed at that first rehearsal with the group. I thought I made many "clams" (jazz term for musical mistakes). A short while later Peg came over to me. She said, without overture "Stella, would you like to go on the road?" I quietly thanked her for accepting me. I was still reeling from the heartbreak of my first boyfriend's marriage. Peg gave me a warm welcome with a firm handshake. I'll never forget that. Daddy thanked her as well. I did go away overwhelmed with this sudden radical change in my life.

I was only 22 years old and hadn't been anywhere. I would

now be traveling with sophisticated people. I was amazed. I was now a member of this jazz group backing the great Peggy Lee. Even though I had never been in a jazz group, I loved this music since I was a child. I recognized the harmonic structure in the standards. That made it incredibly comfortable for me.

My work with Mr. Cafarella was extremely valuable in my work with Peg. It was instrumental in her wonderful, virtuosic jazz musicians accepting me. I knew how to voice a jazz chord through that long tedious study of pure four-part choral writing. I cannot stress enough how important that is in its relationship to jazz. I was given the gift of being able to convey the jazz sound and color. I am ever grateful for it. Without all the ingredients from my teachers I could not have survived in Peg's group. With them, my fitting in with these magnificent jazz musicians was not as unlikely as it could have been.

CHAPTER VI

We practiced hard for one week before opening at Ciro's. I was not one of the swinging, improvising parts of the quintet. I expanded chords, adding color to the music. I wasn't accustomed to "head arrangements." Everything was a "head arrangement," meaning we played the music that was in our heads instead of on paper. We rehearsed with Peg until each song satisfied her both musically and harmonically.

Peg loved glissandos which I normally didn't do except for radio work at ABC. I tried to make sure when we had a guitarist that we complemented each other. Guitar and harp were important for intros and endings of the songs. They cushioned and served as a backdrop for Peg's onstage repartee with the audience. I was described as thus in press leading up to the opening: "Peggy Lee is probably the only nightclub chanteuse in town to use a lady harpist in her act. She's Stella Castellucci, of L. A., who plucks away at the strings of a huge $4000 instrument. The harp weighs in at 120 lbs., just two more than Stella's weight..."

Peg gave me a gown of hers to wear for the opening. It was her wedding gown from her marriage to her second husband, Brad Dexter. She married him on January 4, 1953. He was a very nice, congenial man and a movie actor. Peg had sculpted his hands. She said: "[I sculpt] Mostly hands. I know their bone structure well from wringing my own." She was a gifted painter and sculptor. I saw this sculpture. It showed exact detail of his hands including veins.

Peg and Brad lived in Holmby Hills. It is an adjacent area of Beverly Hills and even more beautiful. The home had what she called a mountain pool. It had an irregular shape because it was made of rocks. It was the only one of its kind I've ever seen.

After getting to know Peg I realized the reason she must have had no reservations in giving her wedding gown away. This was because she was never really in love with Brad as he was very much with her. She told me many years later, that she married Brad because she thought she was going to die. She assumed this because of an illness she had. I cannot recall the nature of it. Her daughter, Nicki Lee Barbour was 10 years old. Peg wanted her to have a good father.

The gown was a beautiful shade of beige silk organdy with a little cap-sleeve jacket. It had a silk taffeta floor-length coat. The ensemble was designed by Howard Greer. It fit me perfectly. Peg and I both wore a size 10 dress. It was so timely. I had nothing other than a nondescript formal. That formal would not have fit in with her style. That was the start of her giving me many gorgeous gowns to wear for her performances.

David Barbour was Peg's first husband. They met while he was guitarist and she was vocalist for Benny Goodman's band. David called her "Pegalee" all the time and she loved it. He was so sweet, quiet and gentle. You wouldn't think he was a jazz musician at all. He could have been a minister or a businessman, but was able to speak his mind.

After leaving Benny Goodman's group they married and had a daughter. Nicki (Nicola, after David's father Nicolo) was born on November 11, 1943. David became an alcoholic and begged Peg to divorce him. He did not want Nicki to witness his addiction. She did not want to leave him but did for Nicki's sake. David would pick Nicki up often for visits. He would take her out when she was a child and teenager. He eventually joined Alcoholics Anonymous and remained sober for thirteen years.

Thereafter began Peg's futile search for new love. She and David remained friends. I saw him several times at her Kimridge Road home. He came for dinner while I was staying there for a visit at her invitation. He remembered me after several years and had always been so kind to me. He remembered Daddy, too. "One close friend believes that 'Peggy loses herself in her work because she can't forget her first husband.' And this belief is echoed by many of Peggy's intimates, who fear that her feelings for this man make it doubtful that she can ever marry happily again."

The nightclubs we played in Los Angeles and on tour were elegant and refined. Everyone dressed in a dignified manner, much different from now. My first time as a musician with Peg was an engagement for two weeks at Ciro's. Ciro's was then one of the most fashionable nightclubs. We opened there on June 19, 1953. "C'est Magnifique" was one of the first songs I played live with the group. Peg sang it in a dreamy way. She enunciated the French words of the lyric with a perfect accent. She performed with minimal lighting. We all got used to playing our instruments in near darkness.

Louella Parsons wrote in her column: "Peggy Lee is so ill she had to skip a night of her Ciro's engagement – and now everyone is wondering if the stork is on the way. Her stint at Ciro's has brought in big crowds, for Peggy's never sung better or worn more beautiful gowns. The night she was off, Dorothy Lamour, Connie Moore and Frances Langford came on from the audience to pinch hit for her."

My parents were supportive of me being a member of Peg's group. Soon after I joined, Mama invited Peg and Brad, Peg's group and their spouses for dinner. We had Latin dance music playing on the record player along with Peg's records. Peg grabbed Louie and danced with him. He was so bashful while dancing with her. He called her "Miss Lee." Peg loved Daddy. She enjoyed talking with him, laughing and joking through the years. They got along so well. After I got established, Daddy came to rehearsals and enjoyed listening.

We had upcoming engagements in Lake Tahoe and Las Vegas. Mama was uneasy for me. She, being Italian but American born in Los Angeles, still was of the persuasion of sheltering her daughters. She asked Peg if Luanna could go along on the tour. Luanna had just graduated from high school. Peg agreed and was glad to have her along. Peg arranged for a nice suite for herself, Lillie Mae, her housekeeper Alice Hanson, Luanna and me.

My connection with Peg happened over time. It really did not take long. Peg was motherly and sensed my inexperience. I would give Peg a Mother's Day gift when we were on the road. Luanna formed her own connection with Peg as well.

Lillie Mae would become a family friend to us throughout

all those years. During "Hard Hearted Hannah," Peg would wear a feathered boa. The song was performed live but it was not recorded. I have a picture of Lillie Mae clowning backstage. She is wearing the boa and smoking a cigarette.

Luanna and I took our first plane ride. We flew to Lake Tahoe for Peg's engagement at a resort nightclub. I was frightened, having never been away from my parents. Nicki and Peg's niece, Merilee joined us there. Merilee's parents were Peg's older sister, Marianne and her husband, Leo Ringuette. They also had a pair of twin boys named Lee and Lynn. I believe they were younger than Merilee. They had sweet personalities like Merilee and their parents. Merilee was a combination of Marianne and Leo. Luanna was helpful and took care of the girls while we rehearsed. School was out and they would be companions.

We all went on a hike and Peg was taking pictures of us. She also had a home movie camera she was using. Luanna and I were used to all the pictures. Mama was a compulsive picture taker. Peg wore a white jump suit with a visor hat and looked great.

Luanna's High School Graduation (1953)

Me & Peg in Lake Tahoe (1953)   *Peg in Lake Tahoe (1953)*

We opened on Friday July 24, 1953 at Lake Tahoe's Cal-Vada Lodge. Peg wore a black chiffon gown by Howard Greer. Joe "Fingers" Carr opened with songs of the "Gay Nineties." We played two packed shows and our set included: "My Heart Belongs to Daddy" and "Lover." I met Nat King Cole there. Peg introduced us when he came backstage to visit her. He was an elegant and kind man.

Peg would later tell Redbook, "Last year I planned six months ahead to attend a week of lectures at a Carmel, California, religious retreat. I drove a thousand miles from a Lake Tahoe engagement, via Hollywood, to the seminar. On my second day, I was called back to work. During the rest of that week, I recorded 24 songs, prepared and opened a new nightclub act at Ciro's, rehearsed a live television program, painted my terrace and started a bedspread for my daughter's room."

The next destination was Las Vegas where we stayed at the Sahara Hotel. It all worked out well and Peg was happy. *Downbeat* wrote: "Peggy Lee who now carries a gal harpist, Stella Castellucci, in her own combo, set for the Sahara, Las Vegas starting August 11." We played nightly shows in the Congo Room at 8:30 PM, 11:30

PM and on Saturday at 2:00 AM. Jose Greco and His Company of Spanish Dancers opened for Peg.

The 2:00 AM show on Saturdays was the one I dreaded. It was so hard to stay sharp but Peg kept us motivated. I got used to it. It was difficult for me being up front. It felt like being ringside to be on stage directly behind Peg. It was that way the whole time I played in her group. I never told her that. I liked Las Vegas least of our tour stops because I didn't adapt well to the lifestyle.

Onstage with Peg's Group for Sahara Hotel Engagement (1953)

My first harp lived in Peg's homes for rehearsals with Peg and her group throughout the years I was with them. Jon Whitcomb, famed American photographer, took a striking picture of Peg smiling behind the strings of this harp in 1954. Peg asked me to leave it there. She would have the movers take it to subsequent homes. I had this harp restored in the 80's.

After a rehearsal Peg asked me to try on her mink stole. I felt so bad having to put it on. She said "If you don't put it on, I will put it right on the floor and you can step on it." I had to do it. I took it home for a while. I brought it back to the next rehearsal. I posed for a picture wearing it in front of our Mount Vernon Drive, Los Angeles home.

We played the Hollywood Bowl Saturday Night "Pops" program on September 5, 1953. Peg was soloist and the first "nightclub singer" to appear at the Bowl. *Hollywood Bowl Magazine* described Peg as thus: "Miss Lee possesses a smooth, sleek prettiness, and in person she offers one of the warmest show personalities in the entertainment field, plus a voice that is exquisite in tone and quality."

Peg was nervous during rehearsals with the prospect of performing with the Los Angeles Philharmonic. The Los Angeles Philharmonic was comprised of 97 musicians. This was the closing concert of their 32nd season. The season had begun in June. There we were, Peg and her quintet on front stage center with the orchestra in place behind us.

This concert was so precious to me. It is the most meaningful event of my career. Daddy was bass trombone player in the Los Angeles Philharmonic. He was seated behind us with the orchestra. He was in the brass section near the back of the Hollywood Bowl's shell. That was his tenth year with them. What a privileged experience to be on the same stage with him. Daddy in a symphonic orchestra and me in Peggy Lee's jazz group!

Rehearsing with Peg's Group for Hollywood Bowl Concert (1953)

Although I was nervous, I was familiar with our part of the program. Peg wore two gowns, one for the first part and another after intermission. The first gown was a white creation of Howard Greer, with a Spanish mantilla. He designed Shirley Temple's wedding gown in 1945. Greer also designed a coral flame-colored chiffon gown for the second part. Peg later gave me both gowns. I would wear them on stage with her. I had a collection. I later gave them back to Nicki and her daughter, Holly. Some of them were used for a collection requested by a museum. Peg didn't require me to wear black as she did her male musicians. She preferred them in black suits.

Peg asked her friend Victor Young to conduct the concert. He was better known for film scores. He worked and wrote a lot with Peg. He composed a piece for the orchestra entitled "New York City Ghost." This stunning piece contained a narration on which Mr. Young and Peg collaborated. This "mood poem" was never recorded by Peg. An instrumental version was recorded by a jazz group consisting of: Herbie Harper (trombone), Bud Shank (tenor and baritone saxophone), Harry Babasin (bass), Marty Paich (piano) and Roy Harte (drums). I worked with Bud Shank many times on sessions and concerts. He was a superior musician, as was Marty Paich. I have completely forgotten the music and narration.

The other songs we played were: "Just One of Those Things," "My Heart Belongs to Daddy," "Golden Earrings," "Mañana," "Too Marvelous for Words," "Legend of The Well," and "Lover."

The album *Peggy* (AKA *Songs in An Intimate Style*) was recorded on September 14 & 16, 1953 at Decca Studios, Los Angeles. Victor Young was arranger and conductor. He co-wrote "How Strange" and "Where Can I Go Without You?" with Peg. We recorded with a string orchestra and her pianist Marty Paich. Peg's recording of "Love You So" I remember well. The melody is running through my head at this moment. It's pure Peggy Lee. I have the original released album all these years later.

The male voice on "Apples, Peaches and Cherries" was Pete Candoli. He was a funny guy, always joking. Luanna and I attended his funeral in 2008. Many jazz musicians were there as well as

John Williams, the film composer. Pete remained a busy studio trumpeter for recordings and film scores.

"Baubles, Bangles and Beads" was from the Broadway production *Kismet*. I love the way Peg inflected the word "gleam" in her singing of "Baubles, Bangles and Beads." She sang it on November 11, 1953 on the Colgate Comedy Hour. It was released as a single. Peg told the *San Francisco Chronicle*: "When I recorded 'Baubles, Bangles and Beads' I thought of a great crystal chandelier with lights shining on it and the whole spectrum of color refracted through a prism."

That Christmas Peg gave me a painting entitled *Virgin in Adoration* by Filippo Lippi. He was Florentine and one of the leading painters of the Italian Renaissance of the late 15th century. It was given to her by Richard Shipman, of her accounting firm Stuart and Shipman. He was formerly a Trappist monk. This work of art has hung in the hallway near my bedroom for many years.

Peg divorced Brad Dexter in January of 1954. Brad later saved Frank Sinatra from drowning while filming *None But The Brave* in 1964. Nicki loved him so much. He died in 2002.

Peg returned to Ciro's for an engagement on March 26, 1954. The Blackburn Twins opened for her. *The Hollywood Reporter* wrote: "Peggy Lee, in her Ciro's salaam tonight, will be backed by a real crazy combo ["crazy" was an often used jazz term for "excellent"], including a lady harpist named Stella Castellucci."

The songs we played were: "That's All," "Let There Be Love," "Baubles, Bangles and Beads," "Why Don't You Do Right?" "Mañana," "Johnny Guitar" and "The Lady is a Tramp." "Johnny Guitar" was recorded on March 1, 1954. It was Peg's collaboration with Victor Young. It was the theme song for Republic Pictures' western film of the same name. It was released on May 27, 1954 and starred Joan Crawford. Peg is heard singing "Johnny Guitar" over the main title of the film.

Peg asked Luanna again to be companion to Nicki and Merilee. This was for our three-week engagement at the Fairmont Hotel in San Francisco. This began on June 8th. San Francisco was my favorite place to work with Peg. It is such a beautiful and historic place. The original hotel did not survive the earthquake there in 1906. It reopened in 1908 in its present state of early 20th century elegance. The suites at The Fairmont were large, with high ceilings. The showroom, called The Venetian Room, had been modernized to a point without losing the old charm.

Peg was having a serious problem with the owner of the hotel. It was possibly about the sound system or the lighting. These were her first concerns. The owner was not a pleasant person. Peg had a room for me in her suite everywhere we went on tour. I was never alone, for which I was grateful. It was a happy time for me, seeing San Francisco for the first time since childhood.

Peg at The Venetian Room, Fairmont Hotel (1954)

Me at The Venetian Room, Fairmont Hotel (1954)

Our lineup was: Laurindo Almeida on guitar, Jimmy Rowles on piano, Andy Lambert on bass, Jack Costanzo on bongos and Chico Hamilton on drums. Laurindo and I played a "head arrangement" of David Raksin's "The Bad and The Beautiful" (also known as "Love is for The Very Young"). This was the theme from the 1952 film of the same name starring Lana Turner and Kirk Douglas. Laurindo and I played this under Peg as she spoke to the audience. Peg and I loved that tune. I would also play themes from Ravel's *Introduction and Allegro* as background music. We used these as segues between tunes.

We made an unusual appearance in the daytime. We played in the Presidio area of San Francisco. This was at a military base for the servicemen. This was while we were appearing at the Fairmont Hotel. There was also a recording session at Radio Recorders in

Hollywood. This was for the Armed Services Overseas Series. I played on that with an orchestra and Peg's group.

The *San Francisco Examiner* wrote: "She [Peg] was taking a shower when I stopped by her Fairmont suite. I talked with Stella Castellucci, the harpist in her act at the Venetian Room. We turned on the phonograph. There was an opera record on top. Then Peggy Lee came in – a picture of platinum beauty, tanned as toast, glowing with good health. She fiddled with the phonograph a minute. Out went the opera and in came Louie Armstrong – soft and jazzy and just right for a coffee clatch."

One of the Fairmont's restaurants was The Papagayo Room. Papagayo is the Spanish word for parrot. It was famous for its Mexican food. The restaurant had its own marquee on a side entrance of the lobby. Luanna and I had never had the wonderful experience of eating Mexican food. We decided to try this popular cuisine on a dinner break. We took Nicki and Merilee with us. The entrance to the restaurant was inhabited by a large number of uncaged macaws. These birds seemed perfectly happy and accustomed to being uncaged. I don't remember seeing any of them flying about the room.

The owners of the Papagayo Room were Al and Katherine Williams. They were a lovely and friendly couple. They noticed that we were looking a little lost when reading the menu. They came over and introduced themselves. They suggested we try the enchiladas. We thanked them for guiding us through the menu. We found ourselves loving the flavors of Mexican food. We all went back a few more times.

We told Peg about the macaws, knowing how much she loved animals. One evening she joined us at the Papagayo Room. On the spot, she bought one of their birds. It was exceptionally beautiful. This exotic bird had brightly-colored feathers. She made arrangements to have the macaw delivered to her after the tour. It arrived at her home in a cage. She named the bird "Go'jus" (gorgeous). She kept it for many years.

The Fairmont also housed The Tonga Room & Hurricane Bar. This now historic tiki bar served Chinese food. The décor included a Chinese boat being rowed in a lagoon. The lagoon went around the entire circumference of the room. There was a bandstand floating in the middle of the water. There were sound and lighting effects to replicate a thunderstorm in the bar. We took Nicki and Merilee there, too.

Me & Peg (1954)

Peg was working on a television show that never materialized. "TV show working title 'Everybody Comes to Peggy's' directed by Rod Amateau. Before scripting the 'pilot' he and writer Bernie Drew circulated around and asked everybody: 'What kind of a girl is Peggy?'" "She currently is dickering for a television show which would originate in Hollywood and would keep her and her modern jazz group on the coast indefinitely."

I caught mumps from a little cousin who was visiting us. After one of the rehearsals at Peg's house I started having symptoms. I was not able to join the group for the engagement at the Riverside Hotel in Reno. All of the group members including Peg and Kelly had to get shots. This was a precaution in case I had infected them. Peg decided not to use a substitute. She was nice about it. She checked in on me from Reno.

My first collaboration with Peg was a song entitled "We." Peg wrote the lyrics and I wrote the music. The song was intended for *The Spirit of St. Louis* (1957). This was a film starring James Stewart as Charles Lindberg. The film was about Lindberg's historic solo flight from New York to Paris. It was directed by Billy Wilder. Peg submitted it for the main title and it was almost chosen.

On August 26, 1954 a poem Peg wrote entitled "The Wounded Mountain" appeared in a newspaper. It was about the brush fires sweeping through the Coldwater Canyon area near her home. Two other poems "So" and "Wheeeeeels" appeared in the *Sunday Times* on December 15, 1954. She self-published her poetry book *Softly, with Feeling: A Collection of Verse* in 1953. I am not familiar with the entire book. I didn't have a copy, but she showed it to me early in my time with her. The title does seem to sum her up in a phrase.

The group participated in The Colgate Comedy Hour on September 19, 1954. Eddie Fisher was host and the other guests included: Louis Armstrong and boxer Rocky Marciano. The appearance was filmed live from the Hollywood Bowl.

Peg then set out for a fall tour. It was scheduled for six weeks, throughout the Midwest and some southern states. The tour consisted of her group, Billy Eckstine and the Pete Rugolo Band. The tour started from New York where Peg appeared on *The Perry*

Como Show ("I Feel a Song Coming On" October 13, 1954) and *The Ed Sullivan Show*, with her group.

In New York, Peg already knew and had worked with the small group of people at previous times. She engaged Joe Puma, a fine guitarist who lived there. She also engaged pianist Gene DiNovi, who lived there. It was the same with the bass player and the drummer. Her regular pianist in Los Angeles, Jimmy Rowles, was ill and could not make the tour. He had been the group's pianist for a long time before I joined.

I was able to meet several of Daddy's relatives during our time in New York. I visited my cousin Ralph Girolamo and his family. They lived on 182nd Street in the Bronx. I met his sweet wife Stella and their four young children: Stella "Tuppie N.Y.", Amelia "Mimi" and twins Ralph Jr. and Vinnie. Stella was Polish and American born. Ralph, with his wild sense of humor, told his kids that they were descendants of the Indian chief Geronimo. They all told their school friends that. He teasingly called them "Wopoles" ("Wop" is a deriding slang word for Italians meaning without papers). He called his wife "Big Stella," who was anything but "big." Peg got a big kick out of my telling her that.

From a letter from Tuppie N.Y. written February 8, 2005:

"I was in high school when you came to New York with Peggy Lee. I was so excited you were here! Everyone in our building, in the neighborhood, on my basketball team and in school knew that my cousin was Peggy Lee's personal harpist! It honored me that Daddy named me after you. So, see: I could never forget you! He had to have thought the world of you. I just hope I haven't let him or you down 'carrying on the name.' It's always been so special to know there's one of us at each end of the continent; at each end of the U.S.A."

Ralph took me to Staten Island on the ferry. We went there to meet Daddy's Uncle Omero Castellucci ("The Maestro" or "The Old Professor") and his family. He was old then and a widower. I met his brother Pindaro, who played in Uncle Omero's symphonic bands, his sweet wife Emma and their sister Serafina. They were all kind, sweet people. Serafina gave me a handkerchief upon which she had added a hand-crocheted lace edge. Uncle Omero composed a composition for harp for me.

Ralph sent me cards for my birthday, Easter, Christmas and many letters. He signed them with some ridiculous and hysterically funny something or other to say, often insulting. Once he sent a huge box weighing nothing, full to the top with shredded newspaper. When I finished digging to the bottom there was nothing in it. Another time he sent a letter on a large roll of data paper with tiny black and green squares on each page. I presumed it had something to say. I unrolled it on the floor and it was all blank. He worked for the New York Electric and Power Co., where he must have obtained the paper roll.

Peg, Lillie Mae and I traveled by train and often by bus with everyone on this tour. This was depending on the locale of the itinerary. The harp was stored at the back of the bus at all times in its trunk. Halfway through the tour we were going through Maryland. Hurricane Hazel hit and we didn't make our destination. We had to stop in Salisbury. Everyone got off the bus. We were arm in arm with four people abreast in order to stay aground. There was a motel where we stopped. It was two buildings separated across a large area from each other. We all watched the roof of the building across from where we were, flying off. It was corrugated metal.

At first the motel manager would not admit us. This was on account of our bus driver Charlie Carpenter, Billy Eckstine and Lillie Mae being black. Peg said that she would not subject them, the Pete Rugolo Band and her group to traveling any farther in a hurricane. She insisted that all of her friends be welcomed.

When everyone got settled in their rooms Peg called the manager. She asked where the nearest market was. He sent someone there to buy fresh chicken and fixings. She cooked a fried chicken dinner on the stove that was in her suite. Cooking oil was spurting all over the small quarters. She ended up feeding the entire tour personnel. She laughed and told jokes the entire time.

Peg was an excellent cook. I learned to love lima beans the way she cooked them. She made them with sour cream and dill weed. Dill is a spice often used in the Scandinavian dishes she learned as a child. As a result of the lima beans, we developed a ritual. Every single time before she went on stage, she always gave a good luck kiss to the men in her group. We prayed, using her word, "omnipresent" (God). One day I said "Good luck, Peg. I loved those lima beans." She laughed and said "Yes, lima beans, that will be our thing." Evermore she would take my hand and say "lima beans" during this ritual.

At the end of the tour we had a recording session. It was at Nola Recording Studios in New York on November 9, 1954. Peg wrote the words and music for "It Must Be So" and "Straight Ahead." These songs were recorded with Gene DiNovi on piano, a rhythm section, The Mills Brothers and me. The Mills were a wonderful black singing trio who started in the 1930's. They were Peg's Decca label mates. The new songs were broadcast over the radio the very night they were recorded.

During rehearsal Peg stopped in the middle of a song. She asked us about the chord changes. The conversation is documented in Leonard Feather's book *Laughter From The Hip* as follows: "'There's something wrong here,' said Stella. 'I have a running F Major Seventh.' 'Heavens!' said Gene, 'and no doctor in the house!'"

Peg, Lillie Mae and I took a train home. Peg was not flying due to an ear problem. She did fly again in later years. My family (parents, Luanna and Louie) waited at Union Station in Los Angeles to meet us. I had never thought of myself as psychic in the least. Coming closer to the station, I had a premonition that they would have a dog with them. They did have a sweet German Shepherd puppy. He hadn't been named yet. Daddy later decided to name him Banjo, after Peg's dog. We had him for almost fifteen years.

We cannot bear to have dogs anymore. We have lost so many through the years. We had them since Louie was a baby. We grieved so much for them, especially Daddy. Louie bonded with Banjo and then together with Charlie Brown, a purebred black poodle. We got Charlie not long after Banjo had joined the family. Charlie had been a prize won at a charity event Aunt Frances had attended. She already had a poodle named Henry Higgins. She gave Charlie to us, much to Louie's great glee. Banjo and Charlie got along well. Charlie assumed the role of "boss." As they grew, Banjo towered over Charlie but that didn't stop him from being the ringleader.

Uncle Omero's composition for harp arrived from New York in the mail. There was a signed dedication at the top of the music in Italian. In essence, it translated: To my niece, Stella Castellucci in remembrance of her arrival in New York. It made Daddy cry.

Laurindo Almeida was a precious friend. He and his first wife, Portuguese ballerina Natalia spent their first American Thanksgiving at our home in 1954. Laurindo told me that Carmen Miranda was not Brazilian, as everyone thought, but Portuguese. They were old friends before coming to the United States. He worked for her in Brazil. He also knew Antônio Carlos Jobim well and worked with him in Brazil.

Around that time, Peg began work on the songs for Walt Disney's animated film *Lady and The Tramp*. She voiced four characters: Darling, Si & Am (Siamese cats) and Peg (a French poodle named for her). She wrote the score and lyrics with Sonny Burke. It was released in 1955.

CHAPTER VII

Peg By Jon Whitcomb (1954)

All of my life seahorses, butterflies and ladybugs have been my favorite little creatures of God. Luanna gave me a gift of two little preserved seahorses. They are contained in a heavy glass bowl surrounded by sea fern. The bowl is mounted on a heavy wooden base with a brass plate that says "Mediterranean Sea Horse." Underneath is a printed history of the seahorse's lifestyle under the sea. She gave them to me many years ago when I was going through a depression. I have mercifully forgotten what brought that on. She saw it in a hotel gift shop where she attended a book signing. She went to meet the children's author, Tomie dePaola.

I love sea shells and have a collection of them in my music room, a converted garage. I keep them next to the biographical books on Peg. I have two matching glass lamps Louie gifted to me over 30 years ago. They hold real seashells inside. Peg's creativity had a lot to do with water, as can be surmised with *Sea Shells* and a song like "The Shining Sea." Peg wrote the lyrics with music by Johnny Mandel. It was recorded in 1966.

The center of Peg's home allowed her to get in touch with water. She always had a pool. The Japanese garden she had at one of her homes was magnificent. It had the traditional red wooden bridge. Peg loved doing her own work in her gardens. She enjoyed planting in the Earth. That was something we both have in common. She lived in four different homes during my time in her group. They all reflected her fine taste in furnishings and art.

Peg shared her ideas with me a month before the actual recording of what would become *Sea Shells*. She wanted to make an album of folk songs, sea chants, and children's play songs accompanied by harp. We started from there and it took shape. There is a note to the listener which is a statement of intent. It is on the back cover of the LP printed in her own unique handwriting. That introduction reads as follows:

Dear Friend,

> Do you remember gathering seashells when you were a child? For me, the songs and poems in this album are something like seashells. I hope they might put you in a pleasant mood and perhaps awaken a fond memory or two.

Sincerely,
Peggy Lee

Jon Whitcomb wrote: "She looked around the small apartment, at the grand piano flanking a record player and a harp (Peggy can't play one, but she's crazy about harps)." Peg wrote:

"Of all the stringed instruments, the harp is the oldest. According to the Bible, it was invented by Jubal. It was used to accompany the Ancient Hebrew Psalms and was also used by David, the poet-psalmist. It was so greatly favored by the Irish poets that it became a national emblem much the same as the shamrock. We used the harp in this album to capture the mood of the sea – and because it's just wonderful to sing with a harp." *Redbook* wrote: "Besides countless popular tunes, she has recorded albums of Chinese love poems, Irish folk songs and old time ballads from all over the world."

Sea Shells was recorded over two dates: February 7, 1955 and March 31, 1955 at Decca Studios in Los Angeles. It took its own natural course. Peg and I seemed to work with one mind. I say this gratefully with no boasting intended. She knew the words to the old familiar folk songs and nursery rhymes. With the exception of the songs credited to music by Sonny Burke, the arrangements were my own. These were either written or done from memory. The arrangements came from rehearsing with Peg when it was just she and harp. Peg explained the song selection as thus: "They were chosen more because of a genuine fondness than for any other reason. The moods and memories they bring, to me, are very peaceful and I hope we agree."

My second harp was also previously owned. Daddy bought it soon after I started my study with Alfred Kastner. It was a style #22 built in 1922 by Lyon & Healy. It is a larger concert size instrument. I call this the "Peggy Lee" harp. It was the touring harp as well as the one I played on *Sea Shells*.

I used my own improvisational glissandos to try to get a sea sound. Peg liked that as an introduction to the opening song, "Sea Fever." A dream-like quality wasn't intentional on either of our parts. Knowing Peg as well as I did, she would find that as flattering as I do. I tried to emulate waves of the sea rolling back and forth. This song came from a book published in 1932 by Silver, Burdett and Co. titled *Music of Many Lands*. She used it for researching old folk songs and nursery rhymes. Kelly found it for her. As it turned out, "Sea Fever" was the only song in the book that was used for the album. It had no indication of origin or country in the book. The music of "Sea Fever" is as written, melody-wise but I arranged it for harp. The lyrics are by Eleanor Alletta Chaffee with music by Friedrich Silcher.

The raising of volume on "Nine Thorny Thickets" was done instrumentally with harp and harpsichord and Peg's voice naturally. We must have rehearsed it that way in accordance with the text. Peg was very sensitive to the depiction of words. There is an emphasis on the line "A fighter betrayed in the thick of the battle." Rolfe Humphries was the poet who wrote it. I don't know if Peg knew him or how he received the interpretation.

Decca rented the harpsichord from the University of Southern California (USC). It was owned by Madame Alice Ehlers. She was a famed harpsichordist and teacher of the instrument there. Gene DiNovi joined us to add harpsichord on the last day of recording. He is heard at the instrument on: "Nine Thorny Thickets,""Little Old Car," "The White Birch and The Sycamore," "Greensleeves" and "Of Such is The Kingdom of God."

On the LP, Peg wrote these lovely words: "Gene DiNovi... who is ordinarily known as an excellent jazz pianist had his first experience with the Harpsichord during the recording of this album. However, being a very talented and adaptable fellow, he quickly acquainted himself with the slightly different technique required for playing the Harpsichord. He seemed to enjoy the experience immensely."

I wasn't aware that "Little Old Car" reflected black humor and a violent car accident. Peg didn't tell me the source of the song. Her personality was funny at times. She loved funny jokes. Telling and being told them (not profane ones). She loved to clown around in the early years I knew her. She was a funny mime. At other times, her personality reflected great sadness.

Peg was intelligent and well-read. She would have been a fine academic had she so chosen. She took great interest in her immense library. Her collection included: literature, poetry, history, religion and philosophy. She was religious and had a great love of God.

"The Happy Monks" is a joyful little song. That is Peg's own composition and lyrics. "The White Birch and The Sycamore" has a medieval flavor to it. I don't know its origin. Peg did not, to my memory, tell me about it.

Dr. Ernest Holmes wrote the lyrics for "Of Such is The Kingdom of God." He was Peg's Minister in the religion of Science of Mind and its founder. Peg was raised as a child and teenager in the Lutheran faith. The music is by Dr. Irma Glen. She was a Minister in the Church of Science of Mind. Peg gave me a copy of one of Dr. Holmes' books. There was no effort to convert me to Science of Mind.

I met Dr. and Mrs. Holmes at a small dinner party at Peg's home. Mrs. Hazel Holmes was a quietly fashionable and elegant lady. She was gracious and good humored. She was a former opera singer. Dr. Holmes was a chatty and humorous little man. He was charming and easy to be around. Redbook wrote: "A neighbor in their [Peg and David Barbour] first apartment building who often sat with Nicki had already routed Peggy to the inspirational sermons of Dr. Ernest Holmes, pastor of the Science of Mind religion in Los Angeles. Dr. Holmes remains her spiritual advisor as well as her closest friend."

In "A Brown Bird Singing" answering on harp or punctuating the vocal was not intentional on my part. Peg and I had a mutual feeling of sympathy when performing together. Peg was happy with the way we arrived at "I Don't Want to Play in Your Yard." The stripped arrangement highlights the lyrics. She loved carousels and music boxes. I tried to emulate a music box in the harp alone section of "I Don't Want to Play in Your Yard."

Claude Debussy's "The Maid with The Flaxen Hair (La Fille Aux Cheveux De Lin)" was arranged for harp from the original piano by Marcel Grandjany. He was a renowned French harpist and teacher at The Juilliard School (for Dance, Drama and Music). Peg requested it for the album. Only a segment of it was used as atmosphere. I studied the entire piece in high school.

Peg had a real talent for imitating accents of all sorts of languages. Peg's Irish accent can be heard on "The Wearing of The Green." Peg explained: "I was interested in older people, some of whom had accents. The people I knew were very kind to me.

Someone you like, you remember how they sound, and many of them are still fresh in my mind." The song recounts a time in Ireland when green was outlawed and could result in lynching. This is the second instance of green on the album, the other being "Greensleeves." Peg was not, to my knowledge, fond of green. Her favorite color was pink. In later years she changed to peach.

"Chaconne (Le Bon Petit Roi d' Yvetot)" is also by Marcel Grandjany. It is mistakenly titled "Chaconde." The title is translated "The Good Little King of Yvetot" from the French. During my interim as a member of her accompanying musicians, Peg heard me playing these solos. She often included them in her nightclub performances.

I love all of the Chinese Love Poems: "The Fisherman," "Autumn Evening," "Going Rowing," "Like The Moon" and "The Musicians." My harp accompaniment was off-the-head improvising on the session. Peg decided to add the poems the second day of recording. She had the book with her, but they were not planned. Peg explained: "They are Chinese love poems from ancient times. They were originally written in the seventh and eighth centuries by some of the greatest of Chinese poets – Li Po, Tu Mu, Tu Fu, and the dancing girl Wu-Hao. These translations are by Peter Rudolph, Gertrude L Joerissen and Soam Jenyns."

The Chinese World wrote: "Peggy Lee, she with the celestial moniker and the nightingale tone, sings at a Nob Hill supper club [Venetian Room]. Just finished Walt Disney's 'Lady and The Tramp' and 'Pete Kelly's Blues' Also waxed some of Li Po's poems with a harp background."

"The Riddle Song" shows Peg's love for all of humanity, nature and animals. She was in love with love. She had great love for everyone she knew or was close to. Peg abhorred racism. She had friends of all races and persuasions. I knew of this great love encompassing all of her work. I felt it in our collaborations. Her four failed marriages were the result of her search for love.

I met my love in the days of the
                                    spring
summer he gave me a gold
                        wedding ring

Autumn he built me a house
              made of stone
Winter he left me to live there
                        alone

I'll bank the fire
from the ~~bark~~ ~~turf~~ of peat
Love's full of waiting
And love's bittersweet

Spring will be coming
And brooks they will sing
I'll still be wearing my
        gold wedding ring –

"The Gold Wedding Ring"

Peg's Handwritten Lyrics

"The Gold Wedding Ring" By Peggy Lee and Harry Sukman
Copyright © 1963 Denslow Music, Inc. Copyright Renewed.
All rights administered by Universal Music – MGB Songs (ASCAP)
Used by Permission. All Rights Reserved.

"The Gold Wedding Ring" is a Harry Sukman composition and piano arrangement. He was a well-known studio pianist. He was Victor Young's pianist and a mutual friend of theirs. He composed it and brought it to Peg's home one day while we were rehearsing for the album. This was before we began recording and happened simply by accident. She wasn't expecting him. It was a wonderful happening. I love the song and the sadness of the lyrics. It is a Peggy Lee song in the finest sense.

As a lyricist, Peg worked fast and unerringly. She did that so many times when writing her own songs. Sometimes on the spot in rehearsal or backstage she would come up with them. She was a voracious reader which made her great with words. Peg had a book she loved entitled *The Art Spirit* by Robert Henri. He was a highly regarded American artist. It was published by J.B. Lippincott in 1930. Henri's spiritual approach to art attracted Peg and greatly influenced her own work in painting. She lent it to me, I read and returned it. Years later I searched for it at Book Finder's stores and finally found it. Another book she loved was *Out of My Later Years* by Albert Einstein.

"The Legend of The Well" was slated for inclusion on a compilation album entitled Classics & Collectibles. David Torreson, President of the Peggy Lee Fan Club wrote the liner notes. It was a beautiful song, to say the least. I know it was ready, but I'm not sure if it was actually recorded.

Nicki recorded her singing debut with the French folk song "Au Clair De La Lune." I accompanied her on one of the *Sea Shells* sessions. It was lovely. She was taking French at a private girls' school. She was given permission to be out of school the day we recorded together. She was 11 years old. She sang with a perfect accent. I don't know why it was deleted, it shouldn't have been. Nicki did not attend other sessions. It may have been one take only.

Sea Shells was not released until three years later simply because Decca got tired of waiting on Peg to complete it. When it was released, she was satisfied but intended to add more to it. The placement of the solo tracks was decided by the producer, Tom Mack, I can only assume. Tom was in the recording booth at all times. He was speaking to Peg and me during the sessions. It's believable about the delay having to do with *Sea Shells* being "too esoteric" for the time.

Peg thought *Sea Shells* may have been "ahead of its time." She told the *Los Angeles Examiner*: "I like the imaginative trend that music is taking today, especially on records that allow the listener to expand in their understanding and appreciation of good music... music that uses instruments, sound effects and voice to create a picture. 'Hi-fi' will help greatly to bring those effects across to the record public."

Billboard on *Sea Shells*: "A quality set of recordings – presenting the chantress in a new light to many listeners. No ordinary pop material – rather, delicate folk and sensitive foreign material, accompanied by harp and harpsichord. The harp gives a feeling of sea and surf. Selections include 'Sea Fever,' 'Wearing of the Green,' etc. Miss Lee's vocals are excellent."

I appreciated the placement of my name on the album cover. I was not at all expecting that. The cover was designed by Decca's art department without Peg's knowledge. I so appreciate her words regarding me. I was 24 years old and my parents were so happy for me. Peg and I did pour our hearts into it. It is so gratifying to know that this could be heard. I am so grateful for being able to be enough of a musician at that age to accompany Peg on this project. I am honored that she invited me and glad I was given the strength and creativity to complete it. It has meant the world to me.

Louie was about the same age as Nicki. The first day of recording *Sea Shells* was only a day after he underwent brain surgery. He was injured between Masses at our church, selling newspapers. Saint Bernadette's had a garden area full of old trees. He was there playing hide-and-seek with his little friends. He ducked behind a tree and stuck his head out just in time to catch a flying rock to his head. I don't know what brought me through the recording but I thank God for it. Louie was growing along with Banjo and Charlie Brown. He was attending elementary school at Saint Bernadette's, where he made his Confirmation. Peg thoughtfully sent a flower and plant arrangement to him at the hospital. It was in a ceramic holder with a figurine of a little newspaper boy.

In the 70's I was called by an orchestra contractor for a one-time concert at the Hollywood Bowl. It was given by folk singer Rod McKuen. I did not know he requested me until he walked up to me during a rehearsal break. He said "You're Stella Castellucci aren't you?" I said I was. He went on to tell me "I particularly asked for you to be in the orchestra for my concert. Before I ever came into the business, I derived a lot of inspiration from listening to you and Peggy on *Sea Shells*." It was a wonderful thing to hear and I told Peg about it. She was delighted. I will always remember Rod McKuen for that.

I didn't know if *Sea Shells* would eventually get rereleased. It had been so long since I'd heard the album. I made time for myself to listen to the entire LP. It brings back so many memories of my time with Peg and her wonderful musicians. They all treated me as an equal, not as a separated female among them. They showed the utmost respect, like big brothers, since I was the youngest. It's great to know *Sea Shells* has been remastered for CD! Listening to Peg's velvet speaking voice on the poems and her singing all those songs was an emotional experience. Those poems and songs are a mirror into her innermost being. Luanna said after hearing it that I should leave it as a legacy to our nieces Jennifer and Julie and nephew Jason. They are three angels who remain devoted to us.

Edgar's original review of *Sea Shells*:

[Peggy Lee (born Norma Deloris Egstrom 1920-2002) was extremely prolific. Hers is a catalogue worth exploring. It covers the bases of so many styles and moods of music. I encourage people to take a listen and let her cast her spell. You will be surprised as you move past the hits and signature songs. She is one of the few artists I can listen to anywhere and anytime. Here, I will take a subterranean look at one of her albums. *Sea Shells* [Decca released 6/19/58] is one of my favorite Peggy Lee albums. It stands out as one of her more experimental offerings along with *Mirrors*.

Sea Shells contains the most beautiful minimalism. Peggy's voice is accompanied by harp arrangements from Stella Castellucci. Stella met Peggy in 1953 when she joined her jazz group. The ladies went on to form an eight year collaboration and lifelong friendship. *Sea Shells* should definitely qualify as one of her masterworks. I think it is an apex of their work together. It deserves a second look. The shapes and colors they made together created music that is eternal. This album takes you somewhere you can go to if you are seeking peace and tranquility.

"Chinese Love Poems" has Peggy doing spoken word. I always love to hear the spoken voice of a masterful vocalist. These short songs induce vivid visions, mostly of nature. The inviting album cover illustrates Peggy as a Venus in Furs. The sea and its shells are not far behind... they are just past her shoulder. There are so many layers, so many "riddles" to *Sea Shells*. Some have washed ashore and some are still buried deep. The treasures will change meaning with each season. While I listen I will keep trying to figure it out. I am ever grateful to Stella Castellucci for providing answers and information. Now, I can dive deeper with a better understanding.]

"*Sea Shells* is a rare, beautiful treasure – Peggy Lee and Stella Castellucci blending their souls and talents to create this haunting, mystical poetic idyll." – Laurie Allyn, June 2012

CHAPTER VIII

Peg played Rose Hopkins in Warner Brothers' *Pete Kelly's Blues* in 1955. Fran McCarg (Edmund O'Brien) is a gangster and Rose is his moll. He books her as a singer in nightclubs during the 1920's prohibition era. Lee Marvin plays trumpeter Al Gannaway. A scene I remember is where she is inebriated, trying to forget her unhappy life. Rose stands in front of the band at Fran's command and can't get through the song. After this, he beats her and she falls down a flight of stairs. There is a scene she plays in an insane asylum with Jack Webb. He plays struggling band leader Pete Kelly. Rose is holding a doll and is quietly telling him about her doll. She is out of her mind due to the brutal beating from Fran. It is then that she sings "Sing a Rainbow," which was written by Arthur Hamilton.

Peg asked me to accompany her to the studio for her scenes. She wanted me to be on the set with her for support. When the film was completed, Jack Webb gave her a large silver trophy. It was shaped like a punch bowl. He had it engraved with his appreciation of her work. She proudly showed it to me. Peg's acting is remarkable. This was her first film since *The Jazz Singer* (1952). She was nominated for an Academy Award for Best Supporting Actress. She deserved to win. I knew the depth of her disappointment in not winning. She sustained her disappointment with her usual grace. It was the last film she ever made. I don't think her ability as an actress was really recognized.

Peg told *The American Weekly*: "I modeled that part on a number of girls I had known. Sad girls, singers who had survived unhappy love affairs and went on doing their jobs the best they could. I love to act. I intend to do much more of it in the future." She would later tell the *Los Angeles Times*: "Whenever I go to do anything, I go all the way. I knock myself out. It has to be that way. Do it or don't do it."

Marty Paich was responsible for my entering the recording session business. Ever since he and I were in Peg's jazz group he would call on me for sessions when a harpist was needed. Marty left the group two years after I joined. He became much in demand as an arranger for many recording artists including Barbra Streisand. I worked on sessions with him until his untimely death in 1995. He had lost his first wife, Hilda whom I knew. They had two children, David and Laura. David was founder of the rock group, Toto. Marty mourned Hilda's death for a long time before he remarried. I felt as though I had lost a big brother. I never had an older brother, being the oldest of a sister and brother.

Señor Wences was a popular Spanish puppeteer. He would appear on national television shows, including *The Ed Sullivan Show* and *The Milton Berle Show* in the 1950's and 60's. He used a funny little doll-like puppet and another stern-faced one that popped up out of a box. The punch line was "All right? --- All right!" Peg mimicked this act to perfection with a Spanish accent and darting eyes.

Peg had a great love for Saint Francis of Assisi (1181-1226), patron saint of animals. She was fond of animals. Peg had a collie dog named Banjo, a cocker spaniel named Lady (gifted by Sonny Burke), a Norwegian Elkhound named Viking and a canary named Joe-Joe. She had the same garden statue of Saint Francis in all of her homes. During our engagement at the Fairmont Hotel in San Francisco, I attended Mass every Sunday at Old Saint Mary's Cathedral. It was located at the bottom of Nob Hill. I found a book about Saint Francis in the gift shop there and bought it for Peg.

Saint Clare of Assisi (1194-1253) was the founder of the Poor Clares. This was an order of nuns doing great charity work among the poor, sick and dying. She was a contemporary, friend and follower of Saint Francis. Peg would sometimes engage me in a little dialogue, herself playing Saint Clare and me as one of her nuns. We addressed each other, as she directed, in a Middle Ages style of speech. This was just a game she invented.

We played at The Sands in Las Vegas with: Georgie Kaye, Don Cherry, Lou Wills Jr. and the Ray Sinatra Orchestra. Ray Sinatra conducted all of The Sands' shows. We were doing three shows a night. Jack Entratter offered his yacht to Peg for her private use during our stay. She would relax on Lake Mead in the daytime before rehearsals. She would dine with Don Cherry at The Patio, the restaurant which was part of The Sands. Don became a devoted friend to her.

Peg appeared on *Producer's Showcase*, a live television special on November 14, 1955. The episode was a musical entitled "Dateline 2." It was about freedom of the press and featured: Janet Blair, Greer Garson, Milton Berle, William Holden and John Wayne. Our group played backstage with the NBC staff orchestra for Peg's onstage appearance. I saw Sarah Churchill rehearsing for a dramatic story presentation. She was wearing a costume of the Victorian period. She was on an adjoining soundstage. She was a fine actress and daughter of the United Kingdom's Prime Minister Winston Churchill.

The Los Angeles Philharmonic made a concert tour of the Far East countries after the Korean War in 1956. It was sponsored by the United States Government. They stopped at US Army posts to entertain the servicemen. Upon his return, Daddy brought back some beautiful oriental pearl jewelry for Mama and gifts for us.

In March of 1956 we had a three-week engagement at the Cocoanut Grove in Los Angeles. Uncle Don and Aunt Nettie came to an early dinner show. This was a surprise for me. They sent a note backstage with a waiter saying they were in the audience. When we finished the show, I went into the showroom to see them. Uncle Don took me for a dance on the dance floor while the house band was playing. After our dance, I watched Uncle Don and Aunt Nettie dance. She was a great dancer. I still have that note.

We recorded a session for *Black Coffee* on April 3, 1956 at Decca Studios in Los Angeles. *Black Coffee* was expanded from its original 10" release in 1953. Originally the album consisted of: "I've Got You Under My Skin," "My Heart Belongs to Daddy," "I Didn't Know What Time It Was," "Love Me or Leave Me," "Easy Living," "A Woman Alone with The Blues," "Black Coffee," and "When The World Was Young." The newly recorded songs for the 12" version were: "It Ain't Necessarily So," "There's a Small Hotel," "Gee Baby, Ain't I Good to You" and "You're My Thrill."

I absolutely love *Black Coffee*. Pete Candoli was the only one on the initial release from my time in the group. I personally think this album shows Peg as the ultimate jazz singer. She has not been duly recognized as such. I especially connect this oversight with the documentary *Jazz* (2001). It was directed by Ken Burns. It aired on PBS in ten parts. It focused on jazz artists, players and singers. I was really shocked with the omission of Peg. If that isn't jazz singing, what is? She could sing a flatted fifth note at the end of a closing chord like a jazz instrumentalist. Peg's talents were not limited to one style of music. That may have been the reason for the omission. She was overlooked as well on the 5CD Set *Jazz Singers: A Smithsonian Collection* (1998).

It is odd that a rerelease paired *Sea Shells* and *Black Coffee* together on one CD. They do not belong in the same package. I didn't understand when I saw it for the first time. The order of the tracks has been rearranged on subsequent rereleases.

Here is a humorous tidbit about *Black Coffee* I saved: "Peg Lee's new record album 'Black Coffee,' has thrown the Nat'l Dairy Assoc. into a tizzy. They frown on drinking coffee straight and claim that the true coffee flavor is only brought out by addition of cream or milk."

I have two favorite albums by Peg. The first is *Dream Street*. It was recorded on June 5 & 7, 1956 at Decca Studios in Los Angeles. This was a night session, as she preferred to record her albums. My favorites from this album are: "It Never Entered My Mind," "Last Night When We Were Young," "Too Late Now" (from the 1950 MGM film *Royal Wedding* starring Fred Astaire and Jane Powell), "You're Blasé" (from the musical comedy *Bow Bells*), "What's New?" and "Street of Dreams." These are all ballads but there's also some great jazz on there. "My Old Flame" was from the Mae West film *Belle of The Nineties* (1934).

Dream Street was made with just her jazz group and Shorty Rogers as arranger. We were doing some "faking" on it. You can hear me playing a "riff" with everybody else on the ending of "It's All Right with Me" (From the musical *Can-Can*). The term "riff" is an important term used from those early days of jazz to the present day. "Riff" is a single rhythmic phrase repeated over and over, usually as a background to the lead melody. It may also be used as a melodic theme in itself. Those musicians were all wonderful. They were as lovely to me as everyone in her earlier groups were.

"Peggy's concern with important details is evident in her choice of musicians for club and record dates. For the recent Sands engagement she had in her group pianist Lou Levy, bassist Max Bennett, Carlos Mejia on congas, drummer Mel Lewis, and harpist Stella Castellucci. 'I use Larry Bunker a lot, too,' she said, 'but he wasn't free to make the trip this last time. Mel is very fine and fits in beautifully. For *Dream Street* I picked tunes I had really wanted to do for a long time. Different things like 'Too Late Now' and 'So Blue.' 'After all,' she laughed, 'you can't play 'Lover' any faster. And I felt a need in myself to do material that would be different for me.'"

"In recent years, she reflected, her work with the late Victor Young was most rewarding musically. 'He taught me a degree of orderliness.' She chopped the side of her hand down on the table – one, two, three, four, as if dividing the table top into measures. 'He'd do that,' she said, 'when he outlined [a] procedure for me to follow. This is the way we'll do it, he'd say. The man had such an orderly mind and was able to accomplish a fantastic amount of work. A shadow crossed Peggy's face as she expressed the opinion that 'so much work probably hastened his untimely death.'"

"In rehearsal, Peggy has an unusual – for a singer – means of communicating with her musicians. She will outline what she wants by means of strange phonetic utterances much akin to those terms employed by the early bebop musicians to express vocally the sounds they created on their instruments. 'Give me a clitter-de-bong,' she'll say, or ask for 'feathers.' The musicians seem to comprehend exactly what's called for because everything invariably comes out kla-bom." Peg once told me that in rehearsal she asked drummer Bill Richmond to create a sound "like a Chinese man walking down the street." He was able to produce the sound to her satisfaction. Bill was cool and laid-back.

During the summer of 1956, I did a series of recording dates for *The Rosemary Clooney Show*. This was for television. I met Nelson Riddle to whom I was referred by David Raskin, a good friend of Peg's. David composed the love song "Laura." Nelson was looking for a harpist. Kathryn Julyé-Gilbert must have been busy. She was his harpist. She also worked regularly for Frank Sinatra. Miss Clooney was married to José Ferrer and pregnant with her second child. She would look at me and smile reassuringly. Once I started playing my nerves would go away. In the years with Peg I wasn't nervous because it was such a small group.

Peg was called to the Flamingo Hotel in Las Vegas in February of 1957. She agreed to substitute for actress/singer Anna Maria Alberghetti when her father unexpectedly died. Her brother Paul was Louie's classmate at Saint John Vianney High School. Anna would regularly headline in Las Vegas. She would invite Paul, Louie and their classmate Leonard DeMonte, to carte blanche in her hotel at her expense. They were three young Italian boys having a grand time.

Peg's sweet sister Marianne was with us in Las Vegas. Marianne was six years older than Peg. She and Peg's oldest sister Della are the only other people I heard call her "Peg."

Peg was married to her third husband, actor Dewey Martin. Dewey approached me with his idea of playing a prank on Peg for her closing night performance. It would take place while she sang the final song "Lover." He proposed that I walk past her in the middle of the song with a long-handled cigarette holder. Since I did not smoke, he would have bongo player, Carlos Mejia light it for me. Carlos would be sitting behind me and pass it to me at the appointed time. It took Dewey the whole day to persuade me to do this.

Just before "Lover" I took the cigarette holder from Carlos. I began to slowly strut across the stage. I passed directly in front of Peg while she was singing. She was in total shock exclaiming "Stella!" I looked back at her on my way to the curtain wings with an insolent stare, as instructed. Marianne was in the wings waiting to catch me. I needed her there. I was in shock myself. Peg could not hold it together and stopped the song. She would normally stand by the piano while she sang. She would become more animated during "Lover." I still have that long rhinestone-studded cigarette holder.

Mel Tormé's California Suite was first recorded in 1949. This is Mel's lyrical and musical narrative dedicated to California. It was arranged by Neal Hefti and Billy May. Peg sang on some of the songs. It was expanded to LP length in 1957. This is known as the "Bethlehem Recording." Bethlehem is the label that released it. It was arranged and conducted by Marty Paich. Marty played piano and celeste on it as well. It was recorded at Radio Recorders in Hollywood on March 11 & 13, 1957.

The full personnel is as follows: Pete Candoli & Don Fagerquist (trumpet), Bob Enevoldsen (valve trombone), Vince DeRosa (French horn), Albert Pollan (tuba), Ronnie Lang, Ted Nash & Dave Pell (woodwinds), Marvin Limonick, Erno Neufeld, Irma Neumann, Paul Shure, Felix Slatkin & Marshall Sosson (violin), Alvin Dinkin & Paul Robyn (viola), Edgar Lustgarten & Eleanor Slatkin (cello), Me & Richard Cornell (harp), Barney Kessel (guitar), Max Bennett (bass), Mel Lewis (drums) and Alvin Stoller (percussion).

My other favorite album by Peg is *The Man I Love*. We recorded it on April 2, 4 & 8, 1957 at Capitol Tower. This album marked Peg's return to Capitol Records. Frank Sinatra produced, conducted and chose the songs. He hired Nelson Riddle to write the arrangements. It was his idea to put menthol in Peg's eyes to make them look misty for the cover photo. I was a "bobby soxer" when the Sinatra craze swept the country. Even though I had grown out of it, I found it exciting to record with him. He kept to himself. I was not introduced to him by Peg, probably because he was uptight.

Peg and Sinatra were good friends. They met when she was singing in Benny Goodman's band and he was with Tommy Dorsey's band. They performed at some of the same theaters in New York. His demeanor was mild and business like. He handled the baton capably. He was able to give cues and "nuances" as though he did it all the time. Nelson Riddle must have coached Sinatra in conducting. He gave every important cue to different parts of the orchestra as though he really knew what he was doing. He probably took charge of everything with Peg's and Nelson's approval. I especially love: "The Folks Who Live on The Hill," "Please Be Kind," "Something Wonderful" (from *The King and I*) and "The Man I Love."

Capitol proposed that I record a solo album. The working title was *Stella by Starlight.* I didn't like that at all. It would sound as though I was serenading myself. The art department at Capitol got involved and pictures were taken of me. Donald Feld (later Donfeld) was an artist there who made a watercolor picture of me at the harp for the cover. He became famous later. He was very nice to me. I selected some standards from Gershwin, Rodgers & Hart and others. It was originally intended to be an album of harp alone with no accompaniment. I wasn't prepared to have other people. They brought in Marty Paich to do the string arrangements at my request. Then they wanted to use electronic elements and sound effects. Marty and I didn't agree with that and the project was canceled.

I played on a memorable session for Louis Armstrong and Ella Fitzgerald on August 18 & 19, 1957 at Capitol Tower. This was for their joint album of songs from George Gershwin's *Porgy & Bess.* The album is a classic and has now been remastered. There was a large orchestra arranged and conducted by Russ Garcia. He was a lovely man and well-known in the music business as a master arranger. He wrote *The Professional Arranger Composer Books I* and *II.* They were first published in 1954. I read of his death in 2011 in a musician's magazine. The arrangements ranged from symphonic to being jazz oriented.

Armstrong and Fitzgerald were ever so modest in their demeanor and kindly to all of us. They had no temperament whatsoever. They just went along with everything, as Peg did except when she had specific wishes. Ella was a good friend of Peg's. I met her at one of Peg's New Year's parties. Peg introduced us. Ella was so natural and nice as if she were not the world-renowned jazz singer she was. She died on June 15, 1996. Louis Armstrong was the most adorable man. Peg attended his funeral in 1971 in Queens, New York, where he lived. She sang "Oh, Didn't He Ramble." Peg recorded her version of this song on the soundtrack for *Pete Kelly's Blues.* This Armstrong & Fitzgerald album is my most treasured recording next to Peg and *Sea Shells.*

The Man I Love Recording Session - April 1957
Frank Sinatra, Me and Nelson Riddle

Recording Session (1958)

I played sessions for Laurie Allyn for her album *Paradise* on October 2, 4 & 5, 1957 at Radio Recorders in Hollywood. I remember a beautiful young blonde who could really sing and express those great songs. Marty Paich was the arranger and conductor. Marty had been Peg's pianist when I first joined the group in 1953.

I did a lot of work for saxophonist Dave Pell. The engineer, Bones Howe, was a character and so nice, as was Dave. Mel Lewis was Peg's drummer while I was in her group before he had his own orchestra with Thad Jones. Red Mitchell, the great jazz bassist, was the sweetest person to me on record dates. Every time I saw guitarist Al Viola on a session, he would say "Hi, comare," which means female friend in Italian. He was Frank Sinatra's guitarist. Trumpeter Don Fagerquist was sweet and funny. Pete Candoli was an eternal clown. He was wonderful both at ABC Radio and in Peg's group.

The great trombonists Pete Carpenter and George Roberts were friends of Daddy's. Vince DeRosa played his first professional job as French horn in Daddy's symphonic band at the 1938 California State Fair in Sacramento. He was "first call" French horn. I worked on many sessions with him.

I received a thank you note from Laurie after her sessions were completed. It arrived from Waco, Texas and is indelibly imprinted on my memory. In it she said that she was thanking every member of the orchestra and everyone involved in her recording. It was one of only two I ever received. The other was from Englebert Humperdinck's manager. Something like that isn't expected in this business. Due to the financial woes of Mode Records, Laurie's album was not officially released until 2004. During work for this book we have become reacquainted and formed a new friendship via Edgar using email, telephone and Skype.

"Stella, I remember so vividly, seeing you, a dark haired slender beauty sitting calmly, your gorgeous hands placed on the strings of that beautiful instrument – so regal. The whole experience was like a fairy tale to me – mostly because of your presence. Thank you for being there then and for the awareness now that you have graced those heart strings with others for all these years." – Laurie Allyn, 2012

Laurie, I am so thankful to Edgar for connecting our paths once again. I appreciate you for remembering me on your album. The selection of songs was beautiful, tasteful and elegant. It should have been released for lovers of fine and really profound renditions of those songs. This album contains favorites of mine: "You Go to My Head," "Paradise," "Surrey with The Fringe on Top," "Easy Living," "The More I See You," and "Where Are You?" Music lovers missed out on a great gift of you singing those songs. I hope you will enjoy a revival of ALL of that passion you have held in check. Sing once again and not just locally, but across far, far distances for many, many people.

I am sorry to say I cannot remember Laurie's brother, Aubrey "Tex" Bouck. He played French horn with Frank Sinatra and with Peg during the *Big Spender* era. In my sessions I must have worked with him. All through those years I was shy in the beginning. It did improve later. I wasn't being aloof but I didn't talk much. At times I would work with a musician and not know their name. I once took a phone call from a musicians' answering service that came into the studio. I called out "there's a call for... " The musician answered "that's me." He was a violinist I had worked with for years.

Peg's group was still playing at Ciro's to capacity crowds. Our lineup included: Lou Levy on piano, Francisco "Chino" Pozo on bongos, Dennis Budimir on guitar, Max Bennett on bass and Norman Jeffries on drums.

CHAPTER IX

McCall's wrote: "Miss Lee does her cogitating and composing in a converted garage – her Cadillac must make do in a carport – which has been warmed over with travel posters, file cabinets, professional recording equipment, a grand piano, a tiny desk and a portable typewriter."

Jump for Joy was recorded on December 20, 1957 at Capitol Tower. Nelson Riddle did the conducting and arranging. Peg was at her swinging best. I can be heard on "I Hear Music," "Old Devil Moon," and "What a Little Moonlight Can Do." This is a really great upbeat album. Peg divorced Dewey Martin in 1958.

I accompanied Peg to the session for the recording of "Fever." It was recorded on May 19, 1958 at Capitol Tower. It was just Peg, Drummer Shelley Manne and bassist Max Bennett. It was so exciting. I think she did it in one take. She rarely did a second take. Peg recorded everything live with orchestra. She also recorded songs for the album *I Like Men* during the same session. She was great at creating concept albums. She would outline explicit details on what she wanted to create. That was part of her consistent artistry.

1959 was the first year of the Grammy Awards. Peg's hit "Fever," for which she wrote new lyrics, was nominated for three Grammys. These included: Song of the Year, Record of the Year and Best Female Vocal Performance. Peg finally won a Grammy in 1969 for "Is That All There Is?" by Jerry Leiber and Mike Stoller.

Kathryn Julyé-Gilbert played in the orchestra on one of Ella Fitzgerald's album sessions. On one of the tunes, the harp part as written by the arranger presented a problem for Kathryn. It must have been too problematic in time to complete the session. Kathryn could fix anything, being the great musician she was. So, Ella in thoughtfulness told the conductor to delete the song completely from the album in deference to Kathryn. In all my years of working on sessions, I've never heard of a recording artist doing that. Kathryn told me this moving story. She remained a fine family friend until her death in 1986.

I worked with Gordon Jenkins for Judy Garland's engagement at the Shrine Auditorium. The concerts took place July 14-18, 1959. He was conductor on Peg's "Lover" in 1952. I was called for the orchestra where I met him for the first time.

Pretty Eyes was recorded on February 15 & 18, 1960 at Capitol Tower. Billy May was arranger and conductor. I can be heard on "I Wanna Be Loved," "Pretty Eyes," "It Could Happen to You," "Remind Me," "As You Desire Me," "I'm Walking Through Heaven with You," "Fly Me to The Moon (In Other Words)," "Because I Love Him So" and "I Remember You."

The day we recorded "I'm Walking Through Heaven with You," Billy asked Peg, "Where did you come up with this corny song?" She said she loved it and wanted to put it on the album. He was good-natured about it though. He was a funny and jovial man. This song is really in the style of popular music from the 1920's or even before. I don't know how Peg came to know of it.

Christmas Carousel was recorded on June 15 & 18, 1960 at Capitol Tower. Peg wrote the lyrics for "The Riddle Song" and I wrote the music at her invitation. Peg wrote music and lyrics for "Christmas Carousel." The only daytime recording I recall was *Christmas Carousel.* Billy May was the arranger and conductor. Dave Cavanaugh was producer.

Peg had one of the first electric typewriters. She must have taken typing in school in North Dakota. She typed really fast without looking at the keys. She allowed me to experiment since I didn't know how to type. I had a fascinating experience trying it out. She let me use it whenever I wanted to. I was just poking along with two fingers. I wrote thank you notes to Billy May and Dave Cavanaugh. Billy arranged "The Christmas Riddle" for orchestra. I thanked Billy and Dave for accepting my melody for Peg's lyric. I received kind replies from both of them.

I became a member of ASCAP (American Society of Composers, Authors and Publishers) in 1960. I was sponsored into membership by Peg and popular American composer L. Wolfe Gilbert.

"Ciro's was packed elbow to elbow for Peggy Lee's opening, and there's only one word to describe this lady of song – GREAT. The parking lot was so jammed that they had to turn away cars, and traffic was backed up for miles on Sunset Blvd."

Cobina Wright wrote in her column: "Exciting Peggy Lee, Capitol Records dynamic recording star, opened a month's engagement before a star-studded crowd of local socialites and Hollywood celebrities. Peggy's voice is suited to rhythm, blues and ballads, and she can pour either honey or red pepper through a microphone with equally stunning results. She never belts – she sings. Her approach to a song is almost like that of an actress."

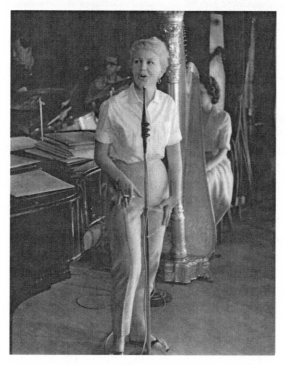

Rehearsing with Peg's Group for Ciro's (1960)
Directly behind Peg: Dennis Budimir (guitarist)
on the left: Bill Richmond (drummer)

August 5, 1960 was Mama's birthday. We were playing two shows a night at Ciro's. I told Peg I was sending my family to see the early show. I asked if she would please sing "Happy Birthday" to Mama during the show and she agreed. Peg called Mama "Annie." Peg sang "Happy Birthday Dear Annie" with the group playing as the cake arrived. Mama was flabbergasted when Peg sang to her. They even shone a spotlight on her. Peg sent Mama a lovely lady's dresser set. It contained a mirror, perfume bottle and tray. Mama was very fashionable. A few years ago I gave the set to Nicki and Holly to keep in their family.

Mary "Penny" Bozocus was Peg's and Lena Horne's hairdresser simultaneously. She was a delightful young woman. I met her when she was in her late twenties. She had a great personality and was often smiling and laughing. She had typical classic and beautiful Greek features with jet black hair. Peg called her the "Glorious Greek." Peg named her doll for Penny in the insane asylum scene in *Pete Kelly's Blues*.

Penny had become ill and was treated at UCLA Hospital. Peg, Nicki, Peg's sister Marianne and I visited Penny every day. We watched her going through the "death rattles" as they were called. We knew Penny was not going to survive. I was standing behind Peg in her home the day before Penny died. I was trying to console her while she was on the phone. She was pleading with Penny's doctor, asking if there wasn't some other thing that could be done. Peg's ensuing crying and grieving was something I will never forget.

Penny was in her 30's when she died of leukemia in August of 1960. Peg had a terrible time of grieving over her. Penny's funeral was held at Inglewood Memorial Cemetery. Peg and Lena were there among others in the entertainment industry. My family and I attended. Peg and Lena served refreshments to the guests at the wake.

Donna Harsh-Benson was the second of Peg's secretaries I knew, and for the longest period. The first one, Hope Colbert was there when I joined Peg. She didn't stay long and moved away. Donna worked for Peg before Hope Colbert as well. Donna was helpful to Peg. She was fun and kept us laughing a lot. She was so good-natured. Peg and I had a nickname for her. Peg started calling her "Diner." Donna married Fred Benson in the second or third year I was with Peg. He was manager for the popular band leader Ray Anthony.

I met Donna's parents at one of Peg's parties. They were lovely people. Donna got her height from her father. She was taller than average, blonde and thin. She kept shorthand notebooks used by secretaries for dictation. They were ever present in Peg's offices in every home. Peg used them as well to write her own memos. Donna and Fred later divorced. She moved away with their son, "Trooper" when he was a small boy. I would love to see Donna again if I knew where she is.

My parents, Luanna, Louie and I were helping to build a large addition to our Yucca Valley home. Yucca Valley is a desert community near Palm Springs. The home was initially small with: two bedrooms, hardly a bathroom, a kitchen and living room. There was no outside porch for shade.

Our dear family friend Bill Pace lived in Yucca Valley. He was an authentic Texas-born cowboy. He was a licensed building contractor. He oversaw the building of a large, L-shaped addition that encircled most of the existing house, which had been built of concrete blocks. Louie helped Bill by digging the foundation for the addition. Louie was attending Saint John Vianney High School for boys. Luanna and I were the water girls for them. We were running buckets of water for them to drink in the sweltering heat.

After the foundation was completed and the concrete walls were up, Luanna, Louie and I, under Bill's supervision, put up the redwood beams in the ceiling of the new living and dining rooms. After the main things were done, the family decided to stay for the rest of the summer and furnish the inside. I helped with the beginning of that but was driven back home by Daddy. I wanted to be able to continue my studio work. I gave up part of it to help with the reconstruction.

I asked Peg if I could stay at her home for the remainder of the summer. She lived with Nicki at her Coldwater Canyon home in Beverly Hills. She agreed and was glad for the company. Donna was staying there as well. She was a wonderful houseguest. It was peaceful at Peg's.

Peg began preparations for a costume party. Donna drove the four of us to Western Costume Company in Hollywood. For decades they had furnished all the film studios with costumes of all kinds. While we were arriving at Western Costume, actor Steve McQueen was pulling out of the parking lot at a rapid speed. I was afraid of even thinking of learning how to drive. I was aghast not only of seeing him but of how fast he was driving. He was known for being a racer of cars and motorcycles.

Peg decided that she, Nicki, Donna and I would all wear Chinese costumes. The ones she selected were really elaborate with full headdresses, as in the ancient custom. These silk costumes felt so regal, as though they were made for princesses. Peg's was a beautiful shade of rose-pink.

Every guest was in costume. Among the attendees were: Steve Allen and his actress wife Jayne Meadows, Jayne's sister Audrey Meadows (Alice Kramden, wife to Jackie Gleason's Ralph Kramden on *The Honeymooners*) and Art Carney (Ed Norton on *The Honeymooners*). Peg guest hosted *The Jackie Gleason Show* twice in June of 1957.

Leonard Feather (jazz critic for the *Los Angeles Times*) and his sweet wife, Jane attended. Jane Feather shared a basement apartment in Greenwich Village with Peg. This was when they were new arrivals in New York City as hopeful young singers. The party was not at all wild or loud. Peg would not permit anything like that in her home. It was just people enjoying nice music by live musicians and dancing by the pool. The catered food was all Chinese.

Summer changed to fall and almost into Thanksgiving. It was a lovely time for us all. Nicki was still in high school at Westlake School for Girls. Peg gave a great deal of parties large and small. She cooked many of the dinners herself when Lillie Mae was not available. She had many personal and career friends who would visit.

In the fall of 1960 Peg's group played an engagement at the

Thunderbird Hotel in Las Vegas. Louie came with Mama to see one of those shows. One evening we had just finished the first show. I was in the dressing room with Peg, her maid Greta and her secretary Mary Bennett. Mary was Max Bennett's sister. She worked for Peg in the late 50's and early 60's. She was a fine help to Peg. There was a knock on the door. To my unbelieving eyes, there stood Father Schnieders with three members of his family. He asked for me. I had not seen him since the talent show at Saint Cecilia's.

Father Schnieders had just seen the show. I was so glad to see him. I immediately introduced him to Peg. She arose from her dressing table. She gave him a warm and welcome handshake. She asked him if he knew Father Spillane and he said he did. She was so gracious and giving of her time. Father Schnieders was quiet and rather bashful for having been Father Brady's assistant pastor at Saint Cecilia's.

Luanna found a turtle on the grounds of our desert home. It was so tiny you could hold it in the palm of your hand. Daddy called her "Desi Desert" after Desi Arnaz. She used to follow Daddy down the kitchen garden of our Santa Monica home every day. She is now just "Desi." She has grown big, about 1 ½ feet long. She is sweet and loves company. She will lay her head on one's shoe if she is close enough. She is a fussy eater but loves: tomatoes, cucumbers, figs and peaches. She also loves nectarines as do I. Her nickname when she is being fussy is "Miss McGillicuddy," Lucy's maiden name on *I Love Lucy.*

I had to make a difficult decision to leave Peg's group. The sole factor in my leaving was that I could not continue, or "keep up" with the rigors and fatigue of touring life. It was wonderful when we were in town at Ciro's, Mocambo or The Cocoanut Grove. It was too much in addition to my studio work. Peg understood. I'm afraid I hurt her in this way. I didn't mean to and regretted it. It did not affect our friendship through all the years after. I was around whenever she needed me. I spent many periods of time at her home keeping her company. She had two secretaries in her last home in Bel-Air. I couldn't do what they did, but I loved doing research for her many academic interests. I liked helping out with whatever I could. I have so many memories of my time with her,

her wonderful musicians and their families.

Christmas Eve of 1960 will remain forever in my memory. Peg invited her closest friends, family, a few career associates and my family (parents, Luanna and Louie). The entry and walkway to her home were lighted with what seemed like a million tiny white lights. On the outside near the front door was a life-sized nativity scene. It contained heavy papier-mâché figures of Jesus, Mary, Joseph and the animals. They were clothed in garments of their time in Bethlehem. Peg made them herself. It was breathtaking and awesome. She hosted a beautiful dinner. Afterward, she had everyone singing Christmas carols.

CHAPTER X

After leaving Peg's group, I continued with my studio work during the day. At night, I was working in string groups at the Beverly Hilton and Beverly Wilshire hotels.

Peg had her engagement in February and March of 1961 at Basin Street East in New York. It was rainy on opening night, as the review said. It was a packed house, overflowing. Cary Grant, Duke Ellington and many other jazz greats were in the audience. Duke Ellington, after witnessing her sensational appearance said: "If I am the Duke [of jazz], she's the Queen." The live album *The Basin Street East Proudly Presents Miss Peggy Lee* was later released from this engagement.

Daddy retired from the Los Angeles Philharmonic after its 1961-1962 season. This was because the mandatory retirement age was 65. Henry Lewis was a member at the same time and played double bass. He and I had been in the senior orchestra together at Manual Arts.

Henry and Daddy got along famously. Daddy was proud of Henry's musicianship. Henry conversed in Italian with Daddy. He would drive Daddy home after the Thursday night concerts at the Los Angeles Philharmonic Auditorium. The building has now been replaced by the Los Angeles Music Center and Disney Concert Hall.

Henry became assistant conductor of the Los Angeles Philharmonic under Zubin Mehta. He later became conductor and musical director of the New Jersey Symphony. This made him one of the first major black conductors. He was married to Marilyn Horne, the famed operatic mezzo-soprano and concert soloist. They later divorced. When I read of his sudden death in New York in 1996 I was saddened.

Louie was elected student body president his senior year at Saint John Vianney High School. The school's faculty consisted of Dominican priests. They were kindly men. However, they were stern in their expectations of the students. It was an important foundation for Louie. He went on to UCLA majoring in business economics.

Louie's Senior Photo (1962)

The Theme Building at Los Angeles International Airport (LAX) opened in 1961. I worked there at The Host International from 1963-1965. This was a unique gourmet restaurant. It is under the two arches that form the building's legs, 70 feet high in the middle of LAX. This location enables a view of the entire airport. I was part of The Enchanted Strings which played every night except Sunday. The violinists would stroll among tables serenading diners. Piano, bass and harp were stationary. We used no printed music, just improvising or "faking."

The *Star News* wrote: "Warner is actually a walking broadcasting station as he directs his far-flung musical group. His cordless microphone picks up the request title and the transistor transmitter sewn into his coat pocket broadcasts it to the compact receiver beside harpist Stella Castellucci in the center of the room. From there the message is relayed by cable to pianist Jerald Linden and Nat Gangursky, the bass player, at the end of the room. All pick up the request simultaneously in earphones."

Me at The Host International (1963)

Valley News wrote: "On busy Saturday nights the Enchanted Strings reportedly grant at least 100 requests, with a liberal sprinkling of 'Happy Birthday' and the 'Anniversary Waltz' to honor the many celebrants. 'Fascination,' they say, is their most requested tune. Two of the musicians, pianist Jerald Linden and bassist Nat Gangursky are Valley dwellers, both residing in North Hollywood. Marty Martinez and Javier Cortes play violins while

Joe Lichter is on the viola. Stella Castellucci, often called 'the angel in the sky,' plays her harp in the sky-high location. As they enjoy the music, diners have an unobstructed view of the jet-age activity below them through the 11-foot windows which surround Host International."

The Los Angeles City Council designated the building a City Cultural and Historical Monument in 1992. The building was closed after 9/11. It reopened after restoration in 2010. Dorothy Victor played one of her first harp substitute jobs at LAX for me. She, her husband Robert and two little girls had moved to Los Angeles from New York in 1961. I met her in 1962, when the American Harp Society was instituted countrywide.

In 1963 I started playing dinner music and teatimes at several restaurants and hotels in Los Angeles and Beverly Hills. I played alone or with orchestras at weddings, art showings, private homes, funerals, balls, Bar Mitzvahs and Bat Mitzvahs. I continued in that work until retiring in 2005.

I purchased my third harp in 1963. The date remains forever in my memory. It was delivered on November 22nd. This was the day that President John F. Kennedy was assassinated. This harp was built by the Wurlitzer Company that predated Lyon & Healy. Wurlitzer harps have an entirely different style of ornamentation than the Lyon & Healy harps. They often have figures of angels surrounding the column and crown. They are reminiscent of the Victorian era they came from and are beautiful. Mine was one of these.

I had this harp until I sold it to Margaret Comer, a dear harpist friend who admired it for a long time. I bought it from the family of deceased harpist Ned LaRocca. I was doing my night job at LAX for which I needed it. I was having the Peg harp moved from there to my daytime recording sessions all the time. I couldn't do that anymore. The timing would be very tight sometimes. The late Vincent Kuehn told me it was available, and sight unseen I asked him to get it for me. He owned Musician's Transfer. They delivered harps and percussion instruments to studios for: films, television, recording sessions and concerts. The company is now owned under the same name.

My family and I attended Nicki and Dick Foster's wedding in 1963. The ceremony was held at Saint Victor's Catholic Church. The reception was in the garden of Peg's Coldwater Canyon home. Nicki was 19 years old. David Barbour attended the wedding. Peg's and David's relationship after their divorce was amiable and loving, respectable in all ways. Nicki and Dick had the most beautiful wedding cake I've ever seen. It was served after dinner under a lace canopy. They had their first child, David in 1964.

In February of 1964 Peg married bandleader and percussionist Jack Del Rio. The marriage was over within months. However, she told me David Barbour (her first husband) was her one and only love. David died on December 11, 1965.

Dale Barco was a master technician who got his training with Lyon & Healy. When he returned home from the US Navy after WWII he saw an ad Lyon & Healy placed. He made many trips across the country to regulate harps and became the "harp doctor." He first came to our home in the mid 60's to work on the Peggy Lee harp. He was the only harp technician on the west coast. He worked out of the Lyon & Healy harp salon on Melrose Avenue in Hollywood. He was a dear man. When he died in 2009, I and so many harpists across the country felt a great loss.

I played in the orchestra for John Frankenheimer's cult classic film *Grand Prix* (1966). Maurice Jarre wrote the score and conducted. I was one of several harpists. The other harpists were: Carol Baum, Marjorie Bundock, Catherine Gotthoffer, Doris Johnson, Gail Laughton, Gayle Levant and Dorothy Victor. I have a picture taken from the *Grand Prix* sessions.

In April of 1966, I was playing for violinist Murray Korda in his string orchestra. We played in the Monseigneur Dining Room at the Beverly Hilton. There was music and dancing nightly. The room was decorated in the Louis XIV style. One evening there was an event in the hotel's top floor banquet room. I saw Greer Garson and her husband Buddy Fogelson seated at one of the tables. A waiter delivered a note to me while we were playing. All it said was "Lima Beans." I knew it could only be Peg. I did not notice Peg and her escort Ali Ipar until then. When the event ended I went over to Peg's table.

Peg and I at Monseigneur Dining Room, Beverly Hilton (1966)

Daddy was invited to join the Honolulu Symphony under conductor Robert LaMarchina. He stayed on with them for 8 seasons from 1966-1973.

Father Schnieders called to invite me to a special event in 1966. It was the 25th Anniversary of his ordination to the priesthood. There would be a Mass at Our Lady of Peace, where he was Monsignor. He asked if I would play for the reception at the parish hall. I told him I would be honored to be a part of his celebration. He wanted to know what my fee would be. I told him I could never charge his parish. After the reception, he presented me with a gift. He gave me a box containing a beautiful sterling silver rosary. It is always in my purse when I travel.

Many years later, I attended Father Schnieders' funeral at Our Lady of Peace. Mama, Daddy and Luanna went with me. He was a much-loved pastor to his parishioners. His picture is on a wall in my dining room. It is displayed among several others of deceased family, friends, teachers and nuns.

The Soft Explosion was a trio I played in with Joe Benson and Darrel Crites. Joe played flute, oboe and tenor saxophone. Darrel played double bass. They were both students at California Lutheran University. They were professional musicians in their twenties. They came up with our name. They were sweet-tempered young men and we got along well. I felt like an older sister to them.

We worked up a repertoire consisting of no written music, just our "head arrangements." We played the Great American Songbook, jazz, blues and Latin. The harp served as a piano. We blended well and played together for two years. We played in public only twice. Darrel got married and became a dentist. Joe moved to Sacramento, California. Some years later Darrel and his wife were killed in a plane crash.

The Soft Explosion
Joe Benson, Me & Darrel Crites

In the fall of 1967, Mama was found to have breast cancer. It shook us all up. She was the first one in our family to ever have the disease. She underwent a radical mastectomy. One of her breasts was removed soon after the diagnosis. She was in the hospital for several days. Our family doctor, Dr. Frederick Hilgert, was a skilled surgeon. He performed the surgery. He called us on Thanksgiving Day morning. He told us the results of the biopsy of the cancerous tumor. He gave us the good news that it had all been removed. Mama was free from this. We had Thanksgiving dinner there at the hospital with her.

Mama was a great driver. She learned to drive on her father's ranch in the San Fernando Valley when she was 13 years old. She took the family around to many places. When Mama got home Luanna, Louie and I decided she should have a brand new car to celebrate her recovery. We went to the Buick dealership on La Brea Avenue. They were having an end of the year sale. We picked out a gray 1968 Buick Riviera, a really elegant-looking car. Luanna and I went to our respective credit unions for loans. Luanna's was for teachers and mine was for musicians. We then bought it for just under $5,000. We decided to add power-locking doors so Mama didn't have to stretch to the other side.

Louie must have taken a bus to the dealership to pick up the car and drive it home. We opened up the garage. We cleared it out to hide the car. The next day we told Mama we needed some help in the garage. We had to decide what we would keep or get rid of. She walked in and said "Well, I thought you had boxes for junk!?" We just waited until she noticed the car. When she did, she started to cry as she always did with things like that. It wasn't too long after her recuperation that she started driving it. She loved it. The car is now in our driveway. Luanna and I intend to restore it.

I met Verlye Mills in 1968. She heard The Soft Explosion. She had been a greatly successful commercial harpist in radio. She started in New York in the 1930's. She moved to Los Angeles in the mid 60's. This was after divorcing saxophonist Arnold Brilhart. They had three sons. Their divorce broke Verlye's heart. She brought her mother with her. I also got to know her well. Verlye became busy as a studio harpist in Hollywood. She played for television, recordings and film scores.

Verlye Mills on the set of The Carol Burnett Show

Verlye played in the orchestra for *The Carol Burnett Show* for its entire run of eleven years (1967-1978). She played in an enclosure. It is commonly used to remove the harp from the rest of the orchestra. This is called a "baffle." It can be glass or a standing screen of some kind for the microphone. It allows a full blend of the harp with a large orchestra.

Verlye invited me to work with her. We began rehearsing to prepare a repertoire of jazz and popular music for two harps. She would become a fine friend and musical partner. In our programs she played the higher register of the harp. I was her rhythm section. I would play the lower and middle register, most of the time. We played Joplin rags, Latin rhythmic songs and ballads from the Great American Songbook. We did work up what was reviewed as a fine, and perhaps first of its kind jazz harp duo.

In 1968 I began playing in Valeria Finzi's harp ensembles. There would be anywhere from 6-12 harpists. We played as a sextet that first year for the Los Angeles Chapter of the American Harp Society.

Each year since her death, the Los Angeles Chapter of the

American Harp Society has held The Valeria Finzi Memorial Scholarship Auditions for students of classical harp literature.

Valeria Finzi Harp Sextet - Concert for Los Angeles Chapter of the American Harp Society (1968)
[Left to Right] Elizabeth Elgin, Dr. Nancy Garf, Janet Leigh Taylor, Valeria Finzi, Joanne Pauli & Me

I took the bus for work until I started driving at 38. I was scared to learn to drive. Louie called me one Monday morning and asked "What are you doing today at 2:00?" I replied "nothing." He said "Well, you're going to be receiving instruction from California Driving School. Please don't get mad at me, but I enrolled you in the course for handicapped people." It took me three times to pass the driving test after the course. I turned out to be a good driver. I only got a ticket once for making a left turn when I was supposed to yield at an intersection.

Luanna and I always shared a bedroom with twin beds before moving to our present home in 1971. It felt so luxurious to have one's own bedroom when we moved to Santa Monica. We began our traditional Christmas tree trimming parties that same year. On average, the trees are fifteen feet tall. They are displayed in front of the tall living room window.

I was an orchestra player for a Barbra Streisand concert at The Forum in Inglewood, California on April 5, 1972. The Forum is a huge indoor venue for concerts and sports events. Also on the bill were Carole King and James Taylor. The orchestra was conducted by Quincy Jones and accompanied all three of them.

Barbra Streisand performed: "Sing/Make Your Own Kind Of Music," "Starting Here, Starting Now," "Don't Rain on My Parade," "Monologue (Facing Fears)", "On a Clear Day (You Can See Forever)," "Sweet Inspiration/Where You Lead," "Didn't We," "My Man," "Stoney End," "Sing/Happy Days Are Here Again," and "People." Barbra's concert was released as a live album. The second time I worked with her was on a recording session. The arranger and conductor was Marty Paich. Her only child, Jason Gould, was very small. He was with her.

I played in the orchestra for *Follies* in 1972. It was the opening production at the newly-built Shubert Theatre in Century City near Beverly Hills. The production ran for a year. I couldn't see anything from the pit, so I bought myself a ticket. I sent a substitute harpist and dear friend, Toni Robinson-Bogart to play the matinee. I played the evening show. I sent my family to see it and they loved it. The music and lyrics are by Steven Sondheim.

The conductor was Paul Gemignani who is from New York. He is now successful in conducting concerts for stage and television. Last year I sent him a Christmas card as a memento. It was the one he sent me after *Follies* completed its Los Angeles run. I do this for many friends and relatives. I am incurably sentimental. The music of *Follies* is absolutely symphonic in nature much of the time, except for the lighter, funny moments in the show. Those scenes have a great jazz and swing style. The score sounds as though a symphony orchestra is playing. It is really beautiful, dramatic and involved.

Motown moved from Detroit to Los Angeles in 1972. I began to work with Motown artists soon after they set up. I played in the orchestra on many of the early Jackson 5 and Supremes recordings. Diana Ross was high-strung, with a sense of urgency to get it done. Other artists I worked with there were: The Temptations, The Four Tops, Smokey Robinson, Stevie Wonder and Marvin Gaye.

I have always admired philosopher Albert Schweitzer. He received the Nobel Peace Prize for 1952. I often quote him in the work booklets I give to each student of my jazz workshops. "Life is for Livin'" from Peg's *Things Are Swingin'* album makes a reference to Dr. Schweitzer. Peg made a sculpture of him. Mama gifted his book *Reverence for Life* to me. She dedicated it:

Stella dear,

God bless and keep you in his care.

Love,
Mama
Christmas 1972

Peg was among eleven selected artists whose paintings were included in the Franklin Mint Gallery of American Art. The exhibition was at Lincoln Center in 1973. She had a true gift for painting. I have seen many of her truly fine works in her homes. Around that time Peg was sent a Tibetan Lhasa Apso dog by the Dalai Lama as a thank you. Peg had performed at a benefit for a ship that brought food to Tibet. Lhasa is the capital of Tibet and apso means hairy. Peg named her Sungi La. When she had puppies Peg named them: Genghis Khan, Kublai Khan and Tibet.

In 1973, I co-authored the book *Rhythm for Harp* with Verlye Mills. Together we composed examples to be played on harp of all the rhythmic styles. These included: jazz, blues, bossa nova, rock, Latin and others. We included original compositions for harp we both composed. We covered jazz harmony in detail. It was hard work but enjoyable. The book now comes with a CD of examples.

As a result, Verlye and I gave the Rhythm Workshop for Harp July 22 – August 2, 1974. It was held at Mount Saint Mary's College in Los Angeles. In June of 2014, Mount Saint Mary's became a university. *Rhythm for Harp* served as a textbook. We had 22 students from across the country. The topics we covered were: Ear Training, Musical Concept (which includes learning to make one's own arrangements), Bossa Nova, Rock, Ballad and Jazz, Technique of Rhythm Playing, Modern Chord Progressions, Improvisation and Special Arrangements of current and standard popular tunes according to student's ability. That was my first workshop experience.

I met several friends there: Michael Amorosi, Peggy Brown, Carmen Dragon, Liesl Erman and Betsey Sesler. Carmen Dragon was named for her father. He was conductor of the Pasadena Symphony. Carmen was an adorable person, magnificent musician, harpist and pianist. She died as a young grandmother in 2010 of cancer. Michael Amorosi was the only male in the class. He got along with everyone well. He was born and raised in Buffalo, New York and earned a master's degree in music from Potsdam State College. He became a very dear friend. He was "the little boy I never had." He is the only harpist I knew who was an orchestrator. For several years he was music editor for a daytime soap opera on CBS television.

I began playing at the Beverly Wilshire Hotel in 1974 and stayed until 1976. I was part of a group with: Harold Greenberg on violin, Ernie Porges on piano and Murray Korda on violin. The four of us worked together in the dining room of La Bella Fontana. We played from 7PM-1AM every day except Monday. I started at 7 during dinner and at 8 they would join me. At around 9, we would go over to the more casual El Padrino Room, which was named for owner Hernando Courtright. Men could wear lounging suits there. Actors Paul Newman and Martin Balsam were frequent visitors.

Murray Korda, Ernie Porges, Harold Green & Me at La Bella Fontana Restaurant, Beverly Wilshire Hotel (1974)

Verlye and I gave workshops and performed together at the 1975 American Harp Society Conference. It was held in June at Concordia College in Minneapolis-Saint Paul, Minnesota. We also performed and lectured for the Los Angeles and San Francisco Chapters of the American Harp Society.

In May of 1975 North Dakota State University (NDSU) awarded Peg an honorary doctor of music degree. That was the same year her album *Mirrors*, one of her masterworks, was released.

Edgar's original review of *Mirrors*:

[I want to look in, to look through Miss Peggy Lee's mirror held with bejeweled hands. The looking glass holds a stash of superb songs. Those regal rings and sparkling things hold it steady. And what does it see? The sterling silver shimmer casts a horizon below the eye down to the beaded gown. Her voice, her majesty is to music what Bette Davis was to the silver screen. This is dangerously close to perfection.

"Is That All There Is?" is one of the most reflective. This can be taken to mean that she is someone who is never pleased, but I think that is totally wrong. To me it is really about the triumph over tragedy. To look back and say that you've made it through. Oh, how right she is about some cats knowing. Some do, even without speaking. They know more than a lot of us.

During the "Tango" there is a snap that occurs from such seduction to sadness and merriment to madness. It is a change of pace as the steps grow faster. "Professor Hauptmann's Performing Dogs" put on a show there in the middle for halftime.

My other favorite is "I Remember." It's too much to take when she says "I remember when you loved me." She should because I only found her two years ago and keep on loving her more. After hearing this album, I was officially obsessed. The album is relaxing, soothing and beautiful. These mirrors won't crack and have already been shining 34 years, longer than I.]

Edgar, you personified everything Peg was, artistically and most importantly, spiritually. *Mirrors* touches upon: her grieving heart from childhood, her romantic heartbreaks and the love she had for her family and friends. Your review and impression of listening to *Mirrors* may as well be a sonnet. It is fourteen lines, as those wonderful sonnets of Shakespeare and Elizabeth Barrett Browning. Peg may have been someone who was "never pleased" merely from my feeling, having known her so well. Yet your assay of triumph over tragedy is probably right.

I love how "Some Cats Know" is revealing of her memories and allowing others to know more than a lot of us. Peg knew a lot without speaking. It showed in her eyes. In a song like "Tango" she could shift with lightning speed from one mood to another in performance, even if it hurt. I could tell from my side view of her, sitting at the harp behind her on stage. Yes, "I Remember" IS too much to take when she says "I remember when you loved me." Please do not alter or delete anything you wrote in your review of Mirrors. Gratefully, Stella.

The *Los Angeles Times Home Magazine* wrote: "Those who know her best are touched by her vulnerability. They see in her poignant expression traces of suffering, the signs of search by a woman touched deeply by life's mysteries and reaching to find answers."

I was a consultant on Stevie Wonder's 1976 album *Songs in the Key of Life*. I brought harpist Dorothy Ashby to Motown sessions. She had just moved to Los Angeles. I wanted to get her working. I told Stevie Wonder to use her for *Songs in the Key of Life*. It happened to the extent that they stopped calling me but I was glad for her.

Dorothy was a quiet, elegant and intelligent person in and out of music. She was a lady, what I call one of the "Great Ladies." Her albums are magnificent. She was also a pianist and had a lovely singing voice. Carol Robbins, whom I knew since she was 12 years old, was a student of Dorothy. Carol was Dorothy's prized pupil. Dorothy kept working until she became ill. She died too soon of cancer on April 13, 1986.

I purchased a harp from Kathryn Julyé-Gilbert in 1977. This was after her retirement. Kathryn was one of the fine radio, film and studio players starting out in the late 1930's in Los Angeles. She came from San Francisco, where she had established a career as a recitalist.

Daddy's 80th Birthday (October 26, 1977)
[photo courtesy of Warren Faubel]

I needed another harp. I already had three but was working simultaneously in studio work and playing steady jobs in restaurants and hotels. It was a gold-gilt style #23 concert grand built by Lyon & Healy in 1926. Like all gilded harps the rest of the body, back and front of the sounding board are made of bird's eye maple and spruce. I call this harp Alfred, for Mr. Kastner. It was hand-picked for Kathryn from the Lyon & Healy factory. It was chosen by her teacher, Annie Louise David, a concert soloist.

Wooden harp columns and crowns are just as good as gold-gilt harp columns and crowns. The wood columns and crowns are a more practical way of maintenance. With these one can avoid having to replace the gilding. Without proper care it will wear off with handling, or become dull. Re-gilding is expensive. The wood versions came out in the 70's and 80's.

While we (Peg's group) were playing at the Fairmont Hotel in San Francisco in 1954, I saw a harp trunk in the lobby. It had Annie Louise David's name on it. I asked someone if she played there. They replied "oh no, she lives here." I was so shy, I didn't look her up. Kathryn would have been disappointed in me had she known.

When I had major surgery in 1977, Dorothy Victor showed up at my home at 4:30 AM for the 7:00 AM procedure. She waited with my parents and Luanna at the hospital. That is the kind of friend she has always been.

I began notating my "head arrangements" for harp in 1978. Eleven of them were published in the *Salvi Pop Harp Series, Vanderbilt Pop Harp Series* and by harpist Faith Carman's FC Publishing Co. These were for: "As Time Goes By," "But Not for Me," "Watch What Happens," "Someone to Watch Over Me," "The Look of Love," "Evergreen," "If," "Yesterdays" (Jerome Kern), "What Are You Doing The Rest of Your Life?" (Michel Legrand), "Like Someone in Love," and "When I Fall in Love." The other harpist-arrangers in the series are: Mimi Allen, Michael Amorosi, John Escosa, Eleanor Fell-Peterson, DeWayne Fulton, Carrol McLaughlin, Verlye Mills and Alberto Salvi.

There were no organized classes for jazz harp until 1978. The first one on popular music and jazz for harp took place at University of California at Santa Barbara (UCSB). It was given by Salvi Harps. It was organized and supervised by Suzanne Balderston. I was invited to be on the faculty with other harpists who were familiar with the idioms.

In my formative years, there was not the help in jazz harp that is available now. Harpists can develop through Lyon & Healy Harp Fests and Salvi Harps workshops. I gave workshops and performed at these events in Michigan, Arizona and California. Now these workshops take place all the time all over the country at various venues. They are usually at college and university campuses. They are not exclusively for jazz but usually include it.

Mine was a solitary journey. I was just trying to deal with all the standard ballads and jazz tunes I had grown up with. I had little time to adopt someone else's style. I do not recommend trying to emulate the style of certain jazz players. I believe harpists can arrive at their own personal style through osmosis, absorbing the music into their consciousness and memory. I hope that eventually they find a place where they feel comfortable in calling upon their own reservoir of color and creativity, playing from their own head, experiencing their own uniqueness.

In 1978 I had a gift made for Peg's birthday. I went to an embroidery shop and explained to them what I wanted. They created a pillow with two female hands clasped in a handshake. One of the hands had a beautiful ring on its finger. This one represented Peg. The other hand was mine. Below the hands are some lima beans. "Lima Beans" is spelled out in green letters across the top. Peg loved it. She couldn't believe it. I still have the thank you card. It says:

Dear Stella:

Thank you for your lima beans.
I needed them!

Love,
Peggy

I love London. I was there in 1979 with Mama and Luanna. We stayed at the historic Brown's Hotel, built in the Victorian era. I saw two livery men in traditional clothing at the front door. They were two elderly gentlemen, one tall and one short, both so sweet to us. We had come to London after a visit to Daddy's family in Italy. We met, for the first time, his three sisters and one brother. We also met their children, my cousins. Daddy and Louie were with us there. This was at his birthplace in Apice, Italy. We also visited: Rome, Florence, Venice and Paris.

Shannon Todd Smith is a friend I met at a Salvi Harps workshop in 1979. It was held at the University of California at Santa Barbara (UCSB). He signed up for lessons with me there. Students have the option to sign up for private lessons. On closing night there is a faculty recital. Shannon lost a lot of jobs playing at restaurants due to the economy. He went to school to become a hairdresser. We regularly correspond. He works at a salon where he is appreciated. He has been such a faithful friend.

We hosted a celebration for our parents' 50th anniversary on November 27, 1979. It was held in our Santa Monica home. We were joined by 125 family members and friends. Cocktails and dinner were served under a huge tented area by the swimming pool. It was drained of water and covered to become a dance floor. All of this was arranged by the caterers. The tables were covered with linen cloths and napkins, candles and flowers. Guests were served hors d'oeuvres, a five course dinner, champagne and a five-tiered cake. The party lasted until the early morning. The weather was cool, but there were tall standing heaters everywhere. Everyone was comfortable. This is another party I wish I could relive again.

Daddy & Mama's 50th Anniversary (1979)

CHAPTER XI

Luanna was orderly as a child and she still is. This put her in good standing as a teacher of 1st and 2nd graders. She was a training teacher for the UCLA Teaching Program. She had many teaching assistants during her career. Mama was one of them. Luanna taught for twenty-five years for the Los Angeles Unified School District. She retired in 1980 after contracting measles at school. She decided that it was the right time.

Louie married Nancy Roberts in 1981. They wed in Chanute, Kansas. That is where Nancy was born. Louie relocated there to work as a computer consultant for the University of Kansas in Lawrence (KU). Nancy was divorced from her first husband and had two lovely children, Amy and Tony. The marriage created a new family with the addition of Jennifer Ann in 1983 and Julia Christine in 1985.

Our parents were still young and healthy to travel. The four of us would take road trips to Kansas to see Louie and his family. In all, we made at least fifteen trips that way. Luanna loved the driving. We all enjoyed the wonderful scenery as we drove through: Nevada, Arizona, New Mexico, Texas and Oklahoma before reaching Kansas.

Luanna took over cooking years ago when we were nursing Mama and Daddy. She never was interested in cooking in her life. It was Mama and me before that.

In 1980 I began work on my book *An Approach to Jazz and Popular Music for Harp*. It would take 2 ½ years to research and complete. It was published in 1983. I started with lead sheets. I had to get permission from publishers to use them. Then I began making arrangements for harp of the standards I selected. These varied in style. I delved into the history of jazz and biographies of jazz artists. It was something I couldn't stop until I finished. I was prompted to write it by harp colleagues and my students.

Beverly Wilshire Hotel – with Wurlitzer Harp (1981)

I wrote a lot of *An Approach to Jazz and Popular Music for Harp* in Yucca Valley. All of the eras of jazz are covered chronologically. The book contains 363 pages exploring the history and performers of jazz and popular music. Topics covered are: What is Jazz?, Ragtime, The Blues, Improvisation, Chord Progressions, Arranging, Tin Pan Alley, Jazz Styles, Latin Music, Faking and Pioneers of Jazz Harp. There are many practice examples, studies and etudes along with 39 arrangements. Also included are discographies and biographies of instrumentalists and singers. Peg is discussed in the section on jazz singers.

Miranda is the name of my publishing for *An Approach to Jazz and Popular Music for Harp*. I was crazy about Carmen Miranda's music and films. She is the inspiration for the name. The book is still used by students, professionals, concert artists and orchestral arrangers. Louie was so proud of me for completing it. He felt that even though I never went to college, the equivalent of this book would have been my thesis for a doctorate. The original edition has a picture of me with a model sitting at the harp. It was taken by Araiz Condoy on a stretch of California beach. It has been reprinted and revised for a 2015 edition.

Michael Amorosi took my manuscripts for *An Approach to Jazz and Popular Music for Harp.* He wrote the music by hand in his fine manuscript. He composed *Five Jazz Vignettes: Suite for Solo Guitar.* One of them, a suite of music in four movements was dedicated to me: "Dedicated to my dear friend Stella Castellucci, who taught me about music." He wrote: "I did this in 1981 – an eternity ago. It's called 'Landscape for Stella.' I hope you enjoy this and you can play them on the harp (If possible – too chromatic, I think). Love xx M PS – Looking this over and the piece we spoke about has given me a nice lift."

I called Verlye Mills "the Charlie Parker of the harp." She could play so fast and perfectly clean. An example of this lightning speed style can be heard on the Frédéric Chopin piano works that she recorded for harp. She was an accomplished classical harp virtuoso and made many recordings. I have many of them including: *The Magic Harp of Verlye Mills* (1956).

Verlye loved jazz and popular music but it was not her specialty. She had some insecurity about keeping a steady jazz rhythm. That is what she wanted to gain from our collaboration. I was happy to provide it. We received an invitation to perform at a World Harp Congress in the Netherlands as a duo. We could not accept. Both of our studio session schedules were full.

After Mrs. Mills died, Verlye lived alone for several years before she contracted breast cancer. After she was diagnosed, her widowed older sister, Mary Ann Roberts, came from New York to live with her. Verlye recovered and continued to work for two years. Then her cancer returned and metastasized to her liver. She smoked and drank coffee constantly. After the liver diagnosis she didn't live long.

I spent several weeks at the hospital with Verlye. That was

when she was alert and still able to eat. Mary Ann preferred that Verlye not know she was terminal during the hospital stay. Verlye was released and sent home to die. It was a Sunday afternoon on October 2, 1983. Mary Ann called me to say she thought it might be the day.

I arrived at Verlye's apartment. She was already in a coma when I got there. Her oldest son was there. All afternoon I played her favorite songs at Mary Ann's request in the next room. It was close to her bedroom. Mary Ann told me that once in a while Verlye's eyelids would flicker and a tiny smile would appear.

It was a long vigil before Verlye died after 9 in the evening. Mary Ann was Catholic. We prayed together after Verlye was gone at the foot of her bed. I knelt there asking Saint Joseph (the Patron Saint of the dying) to lead her into Paradise. The sight of the undertakers taking her covered body on a gurney out of the apartment and down on the elevator has never left me. Verlye was a good friend to me and my family. She, her mother and sister had been to our home many times for gatherings, especially our Christmas tree trimming parties.

In 1984 I gave my first workshop on *An Approach to Jazz and Popular Music for Harp* at Ohio University, Athens. It was followed by an evening solo recital. It was at the invitation of Lucile Jennings, who headed the harp department. She died in 2008 in an auto accident.

Stella Chaloupka-Buscemi was Stanley Chaloupka's younger sister and a fine harpist. She drove to the recital from her home in Virginia. We had known each other since she graduated from University of Southern California (USC) in 1948. Stella died on June 30, 2011.

Arlene Bruno, a friend from Maryland came to the recital. She drove me to Washington D.C. from her home where I was visiting. We visited the Library of Congress. I saw *An Approach to Jazz and Popular Music for Harp* in their archives. We also visited the Lincoln Monument, the Smithsonian and Jefferson's home Monticello in Charlottesville, Virginia.

In July of 1984 Princess Anne, the only daughter of Elizabeth

II and Prince Philip traveled to Southern California. This was for the Summer Olympic Games. It was her first trip to the United States. She stayed at the Beverly Wilshire Hotel. I was engaged by the hotel to play background music for a dinner she hosted. I noticed the Princess looked tired despite her regal appearance. At the end of the evening, one of her ladies in waiting came to me with the Princess' compliments on my playing. She said the Princess had come directly to the hotel from the airport. She was extremely fatigued from the flight. I sent my thanks to the Princess through her lady-in-waiting.

I visited Rio de Janeiro, Brazil with a tour group in 1985. Our group was led by Max Herman, a former president of Musicians' Union Local 47 and his wife. Ann Mason-Stockton urged me to go. The hotel we were booked in was right on Ipanema Beach. It was an old building in the art-deco style of architecture. I was imagining Carmen Miranda walking through the lobby. I loved being at the place made famous by Antônio Carlos Jobim's bossa nova song "The Girl From Ipanema." The food was delicious, especially their famous pure beef. It was served on a flaming sword at the table of a local restaurant.

I saw the statue *Christ the Redeemer of the Andes*. It was overwhelming. I stood at His feet and prayed. We also visited Sugar Loaf Mountain. One can only get there by funicular across the mountains in the air. It was a scary but beautiful ride. I saw Argentina across the mountains from Rio. We flew over the jungles of Brazil getting to Rio. Also on the itinerary was a stop at São Paulo, Laurindo Almeida's birthplace.

I continued coaching jazz harp and freelance work. My deep interest in holding workshops in jazz harp added a new dimension to my career. I was invited as a guest lecturer and recitalist for schools of music at: Montgomery College at Rockville, MD, University of Arizona at Tucson (UA), The Boston Conservatory, Northern Illinois University at DeKalb (NIU) and the University of California at Santa Barbara (UCSB).

In my workshops I have stressed to students to say "I am a musician" and then go on to identify their instrument when meeting people out of the music business. They tend to say "I am a harpist." Harpists seem to get hung up on the mystique or whatever of the harp. They always look surprised but quickly take in the advice. It's in every individual work booklet I prepare for each person to remember.

It was my privilege to be invited as closing night recitalist for the 22nd National Conference of the American Harp Society. It was held in Columbus, Ohio at the Athletic Club on June 22, 1985. I played "Georgia on My Mind," "Spring is Here," "Someone to Light Up My Life (If Everyone Were Like You)," "What's New?," "Dance Only with Me," "Jazz 'N' Samba," "Paraphrase: Bop or Whatever –From This Moment On" (dedicated to Jack Dumont, jazz saxophonist), "Perdido," "Flamingo," and "Constant Rain (Chove Chuva)" (dedicated to Verlye Mills).

Daddy became terminal with Lou Gehrig's disease (amyotrophic lateral sclerosis). I wanted to have more time at home with Daddy, Mama and Luanna. This was for what we were told would be the last eighteen months of his life.

I retired from commercial studio work (orchestras for various artists, television and films) in 1986. I did that for thirty-five years and was glad to be out of it. I didn't feel at ease in studio work all those years. I had regular jobs playing at Trumps, a restaurant in West Hollywood for tea and at the Westwood Marquis Hotel and Gardens for dinner. I would play six afternoons at Trumps and weekend evenings at Westwood Marquis.

I was an invited soloist at the 3rd World Harp Congress in Vienna, Austria. It was held at the Palais Auersperg in July of 1987. I played for "The Harp in Pop/Jazz" concert. I joined jazz and pop harpists: Eleanor Fell-Peterson (USA), Naoko Kubo (Japan), Alfredo Rolando Ortiz (Paraguay/USA) and Harvey Griffin (USA). Eleanor was also Master of Ceremonies.

I played "The Eyes of Love" (dedicated to Dorothy Ashby), "Paraphrase: Bop or Whatever – From This Moment On" (dedicated to Jack Dumont), "Jazz 'N' Samba" (dedicated to Verlye Mills), "Georgia on My Mind" (dedicated to Gail Laughton), "Sunny" and "Yesterday." The entire group of selections was dedicated to the memories of my teacher, Mr. Alfred Kastner and his daughter

Stephanie.

I was invited to give a lecture and play for a master class in Venice, Italy by Susanna Mildonian. She is a classical harpist in Europe and the United States. Susanna now lives in Belgium. I was introduced to her at the Congress by Peggy Brown. Peggy is my treasured friend from Sacramento, California. She was my roommate in Vienna.

I created a poster of Mr. Kastner's European career. It was used for the exhibit honoring renowned harpist composers of the 19th and early 20th century. The poster was a collage of Mr. Kastner's pictures and programs. Ann Mason-Stockton selected these materials from a scrapbook given to me by Stephanie Kastner.

I donated Mr. Kastner's music library to Brigham Young University, Provo, Utah (BYU). I sent it in 2009 for preservation. It now resides among the archives of the American Harp Society. I catalogued it, a copy of which went to the archives. I was fascinated with the original artistic covers by the European publishers. Also listed were their locations, names of the music engravers and artists.

I went with many fellow harpists from the Congress on a hydrofoil cruise on the Danube River to Budapest. Ann Mason-Stockton went with me. We saw the birthplace of Franz Liszt in the Hungarian countryside. We visited the Academy of Music in Budapest, where Mr. Kastner had been professor of harp. The building was intact but going through renovations. Ann and I took the stairs to the second floor. To our disappointment the practice rooms were closed.

After that I went to London and Paris. I had the addresses of publishers indicated on the music from Mr. Kastner's library. It was, for me, a pilgrimage to find those locations and to imagine what the buildings may have looked like. Many of them had been replaced by other businesses. One of them in Paris was a Chanel dress salon. In London I visited the former home of the manager of the Royal London Symphony. This is where Mr. Kastner played Debussy's *Danses Sacrée et Profane* with Debussy conducting for its premiere performance. It was still preserved and served as the Japanese Embassy.

Daddy would walk the whole 2 miles from our home in Santa Monica to the beach. He would arrive at the park at the end of the walk. Mama, Luanna and I sometimes went with him. It was good for his recovery from two lung cancer surgeries. We nursed him at home until he left us one early morning on April 21, 1988. This was six months before his 90th birthday. He was "Daddy" to Luanna and me and "Pop" to Louie.

Our neighbor Nan Merriman-Brand attended Daddy's funeral. She was a former opera and concert singer. In her early career she was a guest of Daddy's symphonic band on NBC Radio broadcasts. We saw her frequently and visited each other. Luanna and I attended her funeral in 2012. She was a dear and lifelong friend.

Dr. Alan Cantwell was a first cousin of Daddy's in New York. He had an uncomfortable hospital residency as a young man. It was not desirable for a doctor to have an Italian surname. The family name was changed from Cantelmo to Cantwell and has remained that ever since. He became a sought-after orthopedic surgeon on Park Avenue in New York. He also died of Lou Gehrig's disease. His son, Alan Jr. has lived in Los Angeles for over forty years. He is a retired dermatologist. We see him often with his long-time friend, Frank Sinatra, who is a second cousin of "Ol' Blue Eyes." This Frank told me that "Ol' Blue Eyes" was Best Man at Frank's parents' wedding when he was 16 years old.

I gave all of our Shirley Temple movies to Louie's little girls when they were old enough to enjoy them. It got to the point wherein Jenny, Louie's older girl would only talk exactly like Shirley Temple. Louie had to send the movies back until she got older and stopped.

Toni Robinson-Bogart was also a member of the Valeria Finzi Harp Ensembles. We played a piece by Dutch composer Lex van Delden for two harps. It was entitled *Concertino* and was in four movements. It was difficult and we rehearsed a long time. We both decided not to go over it again before the concert and felt good about it. The result of going on cold was a fine performance. We played it at the Westwood home of Joan Palevsky.

My Nieces: Jennifer Castellucci-Brady & Julie Castellucci-Durand

In the summer of 1990, I played for a three-month cruise aboard the Crystal Harmony. It was the maiden voyage for Japanese cruising line Crystal Cruises. I was flown from Los Angeles to Tokyo. Then we took a bus to Nagasaki where the ship was berthed. The voyage began on July 24th. I played alone in the same lounge for: brunch, tea, lunch, dinner, cocktails, fashion shows and other events.

My Nephew Jason Louis Castellucci with Lyon & Healy Style #23

Mama, Aunt Carmel and Luanna visited me with a surprise. They all shared a state room. I was playing cocktail music before two lunch and dinner seatings. Out of the corner of my eye I saw something pink coming toward me. "Hi Aunt Tuppie!" It was Jenny. She was 6 years old and flew in from Kansas. She was chaperoned by a hostess on the plane. I asked "What are you doing here?"

I was given a huge cabin with two queen-sized beds, where Jenny slept. Nancy wouldn't let her stay the full two weeks, even though Luanna tutored her. Louie picked Jenny up in Acapulco.

Aunt Norma and Uncle Tony visited me when we got to Costa Rica. This was for the next cruise to the Panama Canal. In Costa

Rica, Mama, Aunt Carmel and Luanna departed for home. Aunt Norma and Uncle Tony would stay the remaining two weeks. They had a luxury suite with a veranda to catch the ocean breeze.

Me & My Niece Jennifer Castellucci aboard Crystal Harmony (1990)

We then traveled on our way to the Panama Canal. There was a fire in the engine room and we were stranded. Some workers were injured. The generator kept us going at a slow speed. The dining room was closed. They wouldn't let me move the harp. They considered it a liability for the instrument. A man played marimba and organ while his wife sang and played piano in a duo. I ran food for them from the buffets on the open decks. That was where all meals were served.

After three days we made it into Panama City. The country that tows you in owns the ship, according to maritime law. The company flew everyone home. Aunt Norma and Uncle Tony were flown to Los Angeles, but somehow I ended up in Atlanta, Georgia.

Tatiana Tauer was a magnificent Russian concert harpist. I met her at the University of California, San Diego (UCSD) for the American Harp Society Conference of 1992. She was a student of Vera Dulova in Saint Petersburg. I saw them play a two harp recital at the World Harp Congress in Vienna in 1987. Tatiana gave a recital in a gothic chapel at the university. It was indescribably beautiful. She had tremendous technique, tone production and musicality.

Afterward, I was hesitant to meet her as I started in classical but was now a "jazz harpist." A friend of mine urged me to get in line to meet her. She asked "You don't feel you can stand in line and meet her?" I replied "I would stand in line and meet anyone... but not her." She said "You're terrible. You don't think you're good enough? I'm taking you right up there with me." When we approached she introduced me to Tatiana. Tatiana knew my name and said "I want to study 'le jazz' with you."

The conference attendees then took a cruise in San Diego Harbor. Tatiana came and sat beside me. She had come to the United States previously to have throat surgery. It was not successful and left her with a raspy voice. She told me "I love the way you play. I have your arrangements. I want you to tell me how to play le jazz."

Tatiana lived a quiet life in Holland with her husband and daughter. In the summer, she lived and taught in Spain. She invited me to stay there with her and give a jazz workshop. She died within a year of that invitation and it broke my heart. She was world renowned. She was a beautiful and caring human being.

I bought my last harp in 1993 from Jack Nebergall. He was a dear harpist friend of mine who lived in San Francisco. He called and asked if I would be interested in buying it. He knew it was the harp that Verlye Mills played in our duo jazz harp concerts. Ten years earlier, he bought it from Verlye's older sister Mary Ann Roberts. That was soon after Verlye's death. This harp is a Lyon & Healy concert grand style #11. Its ornamental style is called "art noveau." It is elegant-looking, not overly ornamented. It was built in 1965. I didn't really need another harp, but was happy to have it for its sentimental value.

Peg performed at Carnegie Hall in June of 1995 for the JVC Jazz Festival. I helped in her preparations for the trip. I was mostly collecting the music arrangements for her accompanying group. These were from her personal music library. It was systematically filed at her home across an entire wall of the living room. It looked like a part of the room, not at all like files, blending in with the décor. The folding doors opened to reveal floor-to-ceiling files of music and arrangements. I say arrangements in the sense that they were written for orchestras and the small groups (such as the ones I played in during my time with her). The group arrangements were for the benefit of the new people. This was useful for out-of-town engagements and for any accompanying orchestra.

Holly may have "New York City Ghost" in Peg's music library. It would contain the score used by the Los Angeles Philharmonic at the 1953 Hollywood Bowl concert. It could be listed under Victor Young. I understand the Library of Congress has requested Peg's music library. I am almost positive this work is included since I helped catalogue it.

The songs chosen for this concert were: "I Won't Dance," "I Love Being Here with You," "That Old Feeling," "What's New?," "Mr. Wonderful," "Some Cats Know," "Fly Me to The Moon (In Other Words)," "Always True to You in My Fashion," "Remind Me," "Fever," "See See Rider," "You Don't Know," "Why Don't You Do Right?," "Is That All There Is?," "Mañana," "S'Wonderful," "The Folks Who Live on The Hill," "Them There Eyes," "A Circle in The Sky" and "I'll Be Seeing You."

Peg went to New York with her two secretaries, Jane David and Robert Paul. Peg received rave reviews for this concert. "The weekend's New York concert top-billed [Mel] Tormé, but Lee, who opened with a 65-minute set stole the show... a heart-wrenching 'I'll Be Seeing You' brought the entire Carnegie Hall audience to its feet, cheering."

I rejoined Peg's group for a few dates in California in the 70's and 80's. One concert was in Concord, California at an outdoor amphitheater. Concord is near San Francisco. After that concert, a note was delivered to me backstage. It was from Elaine Carroll-Smith. She had been in my graduating class at Manual Arts, but I didn't know her then. Ever since that concert we have exchanged Christmas cards.

My last concert with Peg was at the Hollywood Bowl in

August of 1995 with Mel Tomé and George Shearing. This was my first time on stage with Peg in many years. At this performance Peg was in a wheelchair and needed help from her secretary. Peg gave me a black and white silk caftan with long sleeves and a high neck to wear for the occasion.

This was the first time I met Phoebe Jacobs. She was a long-time press secretary for Peg based in New York. Peg met Phoebe when Phoebe worked at the Decca office in New York in 1954.

Eleanore and Howard Cremin were my guests. They got to meet Peg for the first time in the greenroom after the concert. They were thrilled to meet her, having known of my years with her. Peg's former boyfriend, Don Cherry, paid her a visit with his wife. A black man waited a long time in line. He told Peg "When you sing the blues... they're done." She laughed so hard with pleasure. She asked me if I heard the compliment. She really appreciated that lovely man's words.

Peg told me "In your absence, on occasion I have used other harpists. No one does what you do for me." I sometimes had doubts regarding any value I may have had during my years as one of her musicians. Peg's words canceled them. I humbly share them with no boasting intended. I am so grateful that she invited me to play in her group. This was her last concert.

I met Robbin Gordon-Cartier at a Lyon & Healy National Conference I attended in Los Angeles. The day's events were over and people were leaving. She saw me across the lobby and approached me. I was waiting for a cab. She said "Darling, I never thought I would see you in the flesh. I have all your stuff, your arrangements and your books. What are you doing here sitting by yourself?" She was so vibrant, funny and natural. She is a busy harp teacher and performer. She is now President of the North Jersey Chapter of the American Harp Society.

Mama's illness began one day when I was visiting Peg. Luanna and Mama had dropped me off at Peg's house. Peg had not seen Mama in many years. Mama greeted Peg as she was having her breakfast in bed. Luanna and Mama then went to do some shopping. While Peg and I were just sitting down for lunch I got a call from Luanna. She told me that Mama collapsed on our driveway and I better come home. They were going to the emergency room. Peg's gardener, José took me in Peg's car, a black Cadillac Sedan.

Lillie Mae cooked my birthday dinner at home in 1997. Mama was with Carolyn De Costa, her wonderful LVN (Licensed Vocational Nurse). Mama could no longer take food by mouth. She received liquid nutrition through a feeding tube. We saved Carolyn's dinner for her until her dayshift was over. She took care of Mama from 7AM - 7PM. Lillie Mae made a roast lamb and other delicious things. There were ten of us at the dinner.

Willie Andrews was Lillie Mae's helper. He was a lovely and courtly black man. I thought it was sad that Lillie Mae still carried traditions from the "old south." She would not let dear Willie enter our home through the front door. She insisted that he enter through the back outside stairway. Nothing we could do or say would sway her.

Louie installed my first computer in 1998. After he and Nancy divorced he relocated to California and went into banking. He had so much patience as he tried to teach me how to use it. I still have difficulty with certain aspects of this invention. Louie teased me about being able to play a harp with 47 strings and 7 pedals while having trouble with a computer mouse. I had a difficult time holding the mouse steady. He also installed my first printer.

Louie lived in our desert home in Yucca Valley. Mama gave it to him to help him adjust to his new life. It was a difficult time for him. He loved the peace and quiet. The property was 1¾ acres. Louie was an animal lover and happy to share it with his animal friends. There he lived with a Dalmatian and two other dogs he rescued from an animal shelter.

Peg hosted a Valentine's Day dinner in 1998. Lillie Mae cooked a dinner including: baby back ribs, collard greens, black-eyed peas, cornbread and monkey bread. Peg's pianist Lou Levy and his girlfriend Pinky Winters were also there. Thanks to Lillie Mae, Peg developed a taste for soul food much like Daddy. That began when Daddy would travel the Chautauqua circuit by train as a young man. The black ladies in the southern states would await their arrival. They would sell baskets containing a whole fried chicken and loads of cornbread for 25¢. They let their customers keep the baskets.

Peg had a debilitating stroke on October 27, 1998. She would never walk, talk or sing again. Seeing her struggling to communicate was heart-wrenching. She was conscious one year and the last three years of her life she was in a coma. She was unaware with her eyes closed. Nicki would play my *Lights & Shadows* CDs for her. It saddens me forever because I will never know what she thought of them. Her beige and gray cat, "Baby" kept her company at the foot of her bed.

Lillie Mae Hendrick died on May 28, 1999. I played "Amazing Grace" for her service at Saint Paul Baptist Church. She had served as an usher there every Sunday. Holly spoke and Nicki wrote a tribute to her "Sweet Mama Lillie Mae."

Catherine and Dr. Richard Corlin live up the street from us. Their children, Josh and his twin brothers (Andrew and Alex) have become close to us. Richard was one of Mama's doctors. He attended her during her long hospital stay. During one of Mama's times at Saint John's Hospital, Peg was unconscious on the 4th floor and Mama was on the 3rd. Their beds were perfectly aligned. Luanna and I nursed Mama for the last three years of her life at home at night. Mama died on February 21, 2000.

CHAPTER XII

Harmonically, jazz requires intense concentration. You must ask: "where have I been?" and "where am I going?" Knowing the songs and their harmonic changes so well has allowed me to use substitute chords at will. They seem to invite themselves naturally as I work through a tune. I don't believe in random or indiscriminate chord replacements.

I have heard treatments wherein the harmonies of almost every bar of a standard song were substituted. The results were beautifully acceptable. This can only be done by a discerning, thoughtful and discriminating musician who is completely familiar with the song. There should be an element of reverence in this "trespassing," which I hear in the orchestrations of really fine arrangers. Many of them are or were excellent jazz instrumentalists who played the great standards. The recordings and live performances of gifted and seasoned jazz pianists reflect that reverence. I hope my versions do too.

Since the start of my own venturing into playing the standard ballads with a jazz inflection, I have pursued the concept of "less is more." What I want to say and how I convey my feeling for the song come more naturally when I use only the essential notes of a chord. Widely spaced chords with altered intervals, i.e. flatted fifths (-5), flatted ninths (-9), augmented ninths (+9), augmented elevenths (+11), and thirteenths (13), though sparsely voiced, can sound beautifully lush in their transparency.

When I improvise or make an arrangement, "sifting out" the unnecessary notes of a chord has first priority. This process elementally defines the chord. It actually makes identifying it easier whether you're seeing or hearing it.

I learned to "sift" by studying four-part choral writing (Soprano, Alto, Tenor and Bass). The work was long and tedious, but invaluable. It has been pursued by the earliest composers to the present day. In four-part choral writing, you see vertically and immediately, the pure structure of a chord. This study has been the backbone of my improvising and arranging popular and jazz music for harp. I would urge anyone who is serious about playing this music on harp in a tasteful manner to consider undertaking this study. It is a great help in whatever personal style one ultimately develops.

The act of putting an arrangement down on paper is, in itself, getting away from the concept of being a jazz musician. If you are a true jazz player you don't rely upon an arrangement that is always played with the same notes. You treat the song differently in some way each time. The song comes off the top of your head (a "head arrangement") and it often floats away. It will never again appear identically in your memory.

There are now numerous arrangements available. These are good for the many harpists who love jazz sounds. Some lack time, training or courage to become comfortable improvising on the tunes. I would encourage these harpists, though, to use the arrangements only as guidelines in developing their own taste and special sound. That sound will come to anyone who truly loves the music and wants to play it to their best ability.

The *Lights & Shadows* albums are late bloomers in my life. I recorded them after much prodding from harpist friends and pupils. These are the same people who kept encouraging me to write *An Approach to Jazz and Popular Music for Harp.*

I came to the title of "*Lights & Shadows*" for this series after a short time of thinking about it. The songs to me reflected some bright lights and some shadowy ones. The shadows were the "torch songs," so to speak, and are more reflective. I did not go through collections or archives in choosing the songs. I had the melodies and harmonies in my memory. Most were cemented in my mind as a child from listening to Aunt Aggie's piano lessons. These songs by: Rodgers & Hart, Gershwin, Kurt Weill, Cole Porter and many others were simply favorites of mine.

Volume I (released 1997)

"What's New?" / **"One Morning in May"** / **"Spring is Here"** / **"Speak Low"** / **"But Not for Me"** / **"Tangerine"** / **"I Could Write a Book"** / **"Memories of You"** / **"Flamingo"** / **"Meditation"** / **"Love for Sale"** / **"Witchcraft"** / **"Yesterdays"**

Recording Lights & Shadows at Kingsley Gardens (1994)

From the first day on March 9, 1994, until the last day of recording Volumes I, II and III, I wore Daddy's old cotton plaid shirt and cotton pants. That is why I look so masculine in the picture. My hair was cut in the "Italian boy" style for women. I wore only my own thin tennis shoes for pedaling the harp, but Daddy's thin cotton socks. I thought he would be with me throughout in spirit.

It would be comforting wearing his things next to my body. By the Grace of God, I do think it worked for me. I dedicated Volume I to his memory.

When I was recording Volume I, Stanley Chaloupka came to a morning session. He was there at my request to approve of what I was recording that day. He was a strictly classical player but knew what he was listening to. Two of Victor Schertzinger's (Stanley's father-in-law) songs are on Volume I: "Tangerine" and "One Morning in May." My cousin David Hall Jr. attended the sessions and took pictures of the process. One of those photographs became the album cover.

Ronald D. Price PhD, Project Director of Healing Harps wrote: "A musician's musician transcends the commercial, the mundane, and the predictable. Stella's arrangements and interpretations are significant for their transparency, intelligence and reserve! This is a remarkable example of musical maturity – there is no excess. The intent is not to impress by power, technique or device. Instead, every note, nuance, or color has a specific purpose. The listener is gently invited into an intimate milieu. Imagine the special ways we communicate with a close friend, a lover, or particular relatives. This recording is about feelings, memories and intimacy. We are reminded of all those who have loved us. Active listening generates new insights, auditory rewards, and excursions. If you truly appreciate beautiful jazz ballads, artistic interpretation, and the mature balance of the cognitive and the expressive, this is a 'must have.'"

Darin Kelly wrote: "The Castle Light Records release displays so much raw emotion and personal feeling that I felt invasive hearing it even the second and third time around. Castellucci's collections of jazz standards were recorded live inside of a Hollywood bungalow and display the intense melodic drive and brilliant voicing she is famous for. I found myself hooked on every chord change, verse, and chorus. While technically brilliant, Castellucci's playing cannot be described as effortless – I could feel her intensity come through in every chord. Castellucci does shed light on the music, while she herself prefers to remain in the shadows. This music is an emotional, intellectual and monumental statement. It speaks to all musicians (*The Harp Column* Magazine)."

"Lights & Shadows Volume I is an absolute winner beginning to end. This album is solely the artist playing her harp – and the music she loves. Check out the languidly suggestive and sensual "Witchcraft." The approach to this standard is at once unique, daring and completely satisfying. But, really you should give the entire album a listen. It happens to be the most romantic, sophisticated and achingly beautiful jazz you may ever hear. Stella Castellucci is an American Treasure. She is extremely well-known among harpists and studio musicians with whom she has worked and recorded. She has yet to be discovered by the public at large, and remains at the present time, light years ahead of the musical taste curve, like Van Gogh was as a painter. Heaven sent her. Thank God she's still with us. Do yourself a favor. Pick up this album. You'll thank your lucky stars you did. Most highly-recommended."
– Amazon, 2011

Volume II – "A Little Swing, A Little Latin and Other Things." (Released 1998)

"Sposin'" / "Perdido" / "Rose Room" / "Jazz 'N Samba" / "Dance Only with Me" / "Sweet Lorraine" / "Sunny" / "Quiet Nights of Quiet Stars" / "Blues Etude for Harp" / "Rock and Funky Etude for Harp" / "Paraphrase: Bop or Whatever – From This Moment On" / "Constant Rain" / "Have You Met Miss Jones?" / "Whispering"

The cover photo was taken by Phil Fewsmith of the *Los Angeles Times* in 1986. It first appeared in their Sunday magazine. They did an article on local harpists playing at hotels and restaurants. It was taken at Trump's Restaurant in Beverly Hills.

The cat, Scuba, was superimposed by the graphic designer, James Lugo. He did the artwork for all four volumes. It was his idea to make the shadow of the harp look like Scuba. Luanna and I had a small cat as children named Suzy. She ran away twice. We found her after the first time.

Scuba belonged to the sound engineer Aram Arslanian. Scuba kept me company in the bungalow studio. She loved music and remained close while I played. She would curl up or stretch out and remain still during recordings. I found her presence comforting, assuring, and seemingly full of love and approval. In the summer of 1997, Aram found Scuba lying dead in the garden. It broke my heart. I will miss her forever.

Three of my own compositions appear on Volume II: "Blues Etude for Harp," "Rock and Funky Etude for Harp" and "Paraphrase: Bop or Whatever – From This Moment On." The dedications are as follows: "Rose Room" to Uncle David Hall Sr., "From This Moment On" to jazz saxophonist Jack Dumont, "Constant Rain" to jazz harpist Verlye Mills and "Have You Met Miss Jones?" to jazz harpist Dorothy Ashby.

"Whispering" was dedicated to Eleanore and Howard Cremin. This is the only one I did not personally choose in the series. I was told by Dr. and Mrs. Cremin that "Whispering" was "their song." I knew the song but hadn't played it before. They were major supporters in urging me to start recording.

You can hear me breathing at times. It couldn't be removed. Peg liked to hear me breathing during performances. She said it reminded her of David Barbour. She could hear him breathing when they performed together. I seem to breathe harder while playing.

Darin Kelly wrote: "Castellucci voices chords better than any jazz harpist I've ever heard, and could sit in between Errol Garner and Chick Corea without dropping so much as a flat-nine. Her arrangements are as brilliant as her original compositions, which display refreshing originality and melodic flow. The recording makes the strongest case to date for the inclusion of the harp in the family of jazz instruments (*The Harp Column* Magazine)."

Volume III – For Lovers Everywhere... (Released 2002)

"Daybreak" / "It Could Happen to You" / "I Can't Get Started with You" / "Georgia on My Mind" / "If Everyone Were Like You" / "How Long Has This Been Going On?" / "I See Your Face Before Me" / "As Time Goes By" / "Make Someone Happy" / "Paraphrase: A Time for Love – The Look of Love" / "Poor Butterfly" / "The Boy (Girl) From Ipanema"

Most of the songs in this collection as well as Volumes I and II are played with a single chorus without improvisation. Although this breaks away from the true jazz tradition, I have preferred to play a ballad in this style. It leaves the melodic and lyrical statements to rest with the listener. When a lyric and melody soar in complete compatibility, I personally find no need to embellish. It is my hope that lovers of jazz and beautiful ballads as well as the exquisite musicians, with whom I have had the privilege to work, may indulge this preference.

This collection is dedicated in memory of my parents and Sister Catherine Joseph Benton, C.S.J., Sister of Saint Joseph of Carondelet. She was my 6th grade teacher at Saint Cecilia's. "I Can't Get Started with You" is in memory of jazz bassist Red Mitchell. The bass line in the bridge of the improvisational second chorus is an emulation of double bass jazz playing. "Poor Butterfly" is in memory of harpist John Escosa. "Make Someone Happy" is in memory of Aunt Aggie.

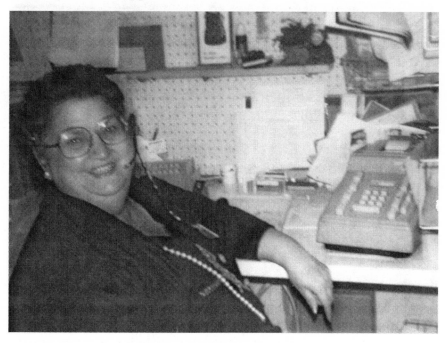

Aunt Aggie
She is totally responsible for my love of jazz and popular music.

I absolutely love bossa nova. This is why I chose to play Antônio Carlos Jobim's "The Boy (Girl) From Ipanema" and "Meditation" (from Volume I). "The Boy (Girl) From Ipanema" was taken from a live performance on June 24, 2000. This was for an American Harp Society Conference that was held at the University of Cincinnati (UC).

Volume IV – For Lovers Everywhere... Part II
(released 2003)

"Dancing in The Dark" / "The Touch of Your Lips" / "The Blue Room" / "Dansero" / "Tea for Two" / "That Old Feeling" / "Come Closer to Me" / "What Are You Doing The Rest of Your Life?" / "I'm Old Fashioned" / "Thee I Love" / "All The Things You Are" / "Snowfall" / "On Green Dolphin Street" / "The Very Thought of You" / "The Man I Love" / "While We're Young"

In the continuation of *Lights & Shadows – For Lovers Everywhere*, most of the songs are again played with only one chorus, without improvisation. I think of these one chorus treatments as little essays wherein the melody line remains as written and faithful to the lyric.

Some ballads, for me, come under the heading of "profound" songs. The compelling architecture uniting a beautiful melody with a moving lyric is, to my mind, a profound song. I have always felt this way about "All The Things You Are," "The Touch of Your Lips," "The Very Thought of You," and "While We're Young," among others. "While We're Young" as treated here is almost entirely one-on-one, a single melody note over a single accompanying note. I hope these little essays, from this humble player and lover of jazz and beautiful ballads may find a place in your love of jazz and beautiful love songs.

This collection is dedicated in memory of Mary Rose Estrada, sweet sister-in-law, Michael Amorosi, loyal friend and cherished pupil and Alfred Kastner, venerable teacher. In the liner notes is a picture of my nephew Jason Castellucci with his younger cousin Julian Madison as children. Julian is the grandson of Mary Rose Estrada. She is on the cover. "Dancing in The Dark" is dedicated to her.

After I played Mary Rose's funeral, I prayed. I asked her to please help me from Heaven to get through Volume IV. I was surprised when I got the first box of CDs. On the back cover, James Lugo had placed Mary Rose's white hat on top of the harp. It was my symbolic way of saying I am "hanging up my hat" for recording. For a time I was considering Volume V. As time passes I am prone to thinking I would like to stop there.

The other dedications are: "Dansero" to Michael Amorosi, "Tea for Two" to Mama, "Come Closer to Me" (Acercate Mas) to the Silveyra, Longoria and Estrada families, "Snowfall" to my dear cousin David Hall Jr. for his steadfast encouragement and "While We're Young" to precious friend and "Big Sister" Miss Peggy Lee.

When playing "Tea for Two" I like to use a segment of "Limehouse Blues." In the film *Ziegfeld Follies* (1946), Fred Astaire dances to it with Lucille Bremer. Lime Street was in the Chinatown sector of old London. Young Chinese girls worked there as prostitutes. The lyrics by Douglas Furber allude to that. I made the connection with tea and China. I also like to work history in when I can.

I was, and still am, surprised by the reviews I received. I was really overwhelmed by the words of Ronald D. Price and Darin Kelly. I told them so, by letter and email. They made me wish Daddy had been alive to see them. He would have been proud of his daughter who always thought she wasn't good enough. He often preached to me about that. Darin Kelly is a trumpeter. I told him how proud Daddy would have been. Daddy most likely would have said "Didn't I tell you? And it came from a brass man." I get feedback about the relaxing atmosphere of the CDs from: doctors, massage therapists, people reading and doing research. I am eternally grateful and gratified.

These recordings were labors of love. It was agonizing over the five month period it took to complete Volumes I-III. There were long periods in between the sessions. Those were recorded March through September of 1994 at Kingsley Gardens in Hollywood. This bungalow studio is owned by Aram Arslanian. Volume IV was produced, recorded, mixed and mastered by Buddy Halligan. He is married to jazz harpist Carol Robbins. This was the only one recorded in a soundproof recording studio, Bell Sound Studios in Hollywood. The entire series contains thirty-nine standards and three originals.

CHAPTER XIII

Michael Amorosi left Los Angeles to die in Grand Island, New York. He died on February 26, 2000. This was five days after Mama. He taught music at West Hertel Middle School in New York. He was so adorable. I have his picture on the mantle in my room along with dried roses. He sent them to one of my recitals in the 90's. I received my first Mother's Day card ever from his sister, Deborah in 2013. I told her what Michael meant to me and we became friends through email.

Michael Amorosi
My cherished friend, pupil and "the little boy I never had."

Aïda Mulieri-Dagort, my first teacher, was a good friend. She died of cancer on June 9, 2000. I played her funeral at the request of her husband, Vincent and son, Philip. Her coffin was the most beautiful I have ever seen. It was made of rare carved wood and designed by Philip. It had harp motifs in the most elegant and subtle manner. She was buried at Riverside National Cemetery in Riverside, California. She is buried there because her husband Vincent is a WWII veteran.

Aïda held a Bachelor's Degree in Education from UCLA, in addition to being a major in Music. She played harp for Paramount and Warner Brothers Studio orchestras. She retired because of arthritis in her hands. She took up painting in a serious way. She painted oils, watercolors and other forms. I have a pair of watercolors she gifted me of Mission San Fernando Rey de España. That is one of many historic missions in California founded by Father Junípero Serra in 1768. He was a Franciscan priest who traveled by foot throughout the state. She lived near there and painted the mission pictures at the site. They have hung in our living room for many years now. Luanna and I have traveled to many of the missions.

I didn't see much of Aïda after she and Vincent moved near Palm Springs. Her autobiography *Harps Are Not for Angels* was published in 1997. I still think of her when I see films scored by Elmer Bernstein. One of those is *To Kill a Mocking Bird* (1962). It must be Aïda playing. She played for all of Bernstein's sessions.

When Philip was a child he was a talented magician. Aïda would take him to children's birthday parties and other related events to perform. She was proud of him. As an adult, he is an interior decorator and is in demand in related fields. He was here for dinner about a year ago. We have remained in touch. Vincent still lives in Rancho Mirage, a popular and stylish desert community. Luanna, Louie and I attended his 90th birthday party at their country club. Aïda was missed so much.

I became a member of the faculty for Susan Allen's Summer Harp Course in 2001. This was a master class held by the California Institute of The Arts. Susan is assistant dean of music and heads the harp department there. This two-week course took place annually. It was for harpists of all ages and levels. My specialty was in jazz harp. I brought my Wurlitzer and Verlye's style #11. I continued this for many summers. The grounds were in the Pacific Palisades and resembled a forest. My first faculty recital for Susan's course was held in a redwood chapel. It originally belonged to a Methodist Church. It has since been used as a venue for group meetings, weddings and by monks for study and contemplation.

Peggy Lee was a luminous and fine singer of jazz and beautiful ballads. She taught me so much about having a balanced life. She said "I am guided in life by the grand essentials: something to do, something to love and something to hope for." Her schedules allowed time for: spirituality, two to three months of tours, recordings and long periods of time at home. She did all of her own interior decorating and gardening. The dishes she cooked were innovative palate pleasers.

My family loved Peg and she loved them. Peg remained a close family friend to my parents, Luanna, Louie and me until the end of her life. I was privileged to play harp in the jazz quintets and sextets accompanying her for eight years. I got to know and appreciate her. She was a beautiful, sensitive human being and faithful friend. She was concerned with everyone's welfare. Peg was a "Big Sister" to me in the truest sense of the word.

When Peg died on January 21, 2002, Nicki asked me to play for the ash burial ceremony. This was held at Westwood Memorial Park. Nicki wanted only harp at the site wherein was a beautiful marble bench. The bench was opened for interring the ashes. Inscribed on the surface is "Music is my life's breath" and "Angels on your pillow, Mama Peggy." "Mama Peggy" is what her three grandchildren called her. "Angels on Your Pillow" was a song from *Peg*, her autobiographical musical. It had a brief run on Broadway in 1983. I don't know why it was not successful, I never saw it. She didn't speak to me about it. I heard someone say that it carried too much sadness. "Peg" is what I always called her merely by instinct and she never objected.

There was just a small group in attendance at the ash burial: the family, two career associates, a minister, one of her doctors and his wife. There is a "Peggy Lee Rose" bush next to the bench. Peg's gardener, José, planted it from Peg's own garden. The roses are of course, pink and are listed with the American Rose Society. Peg's bench is just across from the marble wall in which Mama's ashes are interred. Later the family cleared Peg's Bel-Air home. Nicki knew about the "Lima Beans" pillow and recognized it. She and Holly mailed it to me.

Susan Allen presented another of my solo recitals on July 27, 2004 at the Pacific Palisades Women's Club. Recitals were moved there because of the noise from outside traffic. I played "While We're Young." This 1943 Alec Wilder song was dedicated to Peg in my program. It was one of her favorite songs. Peg met Alec Wilder while she was in Benny Goodman's band. I dedicated "I Can't Get Started with You" (Gershwin) to jazz bassist Red Mitchell. A part of the second chorus was an improvisation on a jazz double bass line.

Ann Mason-Stockton lived in a condominium in Westwood, an area of Los Angeles near Beverly Hills and UCLA, her alma mater. I sat next to her bed as she was dying in her room the afternoon of August 11, 2006. It was an unreal experience to see this tiny woman in a coma. She was always active working in the studios. She was a board member and one-term president of the American Harp Society from 1976-1980. She became a close friend to our entire family.

At Ann's memorial service, I played two of her favorite songs from *Lights & Shadows*. She requested: "Daybreak" (1926) [Music - Ferde Grofé / Lyrics - Harold Adamson] and "Poor Butterfly" (1916) [Music - Raymond Hubbel / Lyrics - J.L. Golden]. If she had not asked me five years before her death, I would not have had the strength to play for her at all. I know she was right there pulling me through.

Luanna and I hosted a reception and luncheon at our home in October of 2006. It was attended by harpists from the Los Angeles Chapter of the American Harp Society and Ann's musician friends from the film studios. It was outside in the courtyard and other garden areas. Thanks to clement weather, the atmosphere was a happy one, as Ann would have wanted. Ann's daughter Martha, son-in-law and two granddaughters were there. I remember when Martha was born in 1948.

Ann Mason-Stockton

The only sad element at Ann's memorial reception was her son David's absence. He died a few years previously from drowning. He was a Vietnam veteran and lived in Michigan with his wife. His ashes are interred next to his parents and his maternal grandmother, Elva Bartlett Mason. They all rest in Westwood Memorial Park. This is the same resting place of Mama and Peg.

Jascha Heifetz (1901-1987) specifically requested Ann for a recording. She played the harp part on a work for violin and orchestra entitled *Scottish Fantasy*. It was composed by Max Bruch. She also made several of her own classical harp recordings of which I have.

Ann was in the contract orchestra for 20th Century-Fox for over thirty years. She would end up playing on over 800 film scores including: *Gone With The Wind* (1939) and Steven Spielberg's *Schindler's List* (1993). At her invitation, I played on a few of them with her. These included: *20,000 Leagues Under The Sea* (1954), *The Diary of Anne Frank* (1959), *Camelot* (1967) and *Jaws 2*

(1978). This was when more than one harp was in the orchestra score. *Jaws 2*, for example was: Ann, Catherine Gotthoffer, Dorothy Remsen and me. In 2006, Ann received the American Harp Society Lifetime Achievement Award. NPR (National Public Radio) in Los Angeles announced Ann's death and played an excerpt from one of her recordings.

Peter Richmond contacted me about the book he was writing, *Fever – The Life and Music of Miss Peggy Lee*. He came to my home for interviews and lunches. What is hurtful is that he offered (without my asking), to send a copy of his book upon its release. That didn't happen. Phoebe Jacobs sent it to me from New York out of the blue. It was just like Phoebe to do such a thoughtful thing. Phoebe was a dear friend to me until her passing on April 9, 2012. She was a straight-ahead and strong businesswoman.

Luanna and I were periodically involved in caregiving for our dear Aunt Carmel DeLellis-Hall. We had known her since we were babies. She lived in Ventura, 60 miles from Santa Monica. She lived in a gated beach community. Her home had no backyard, just a large deck overlooking the Pacific Ocean. It was only a few yards away. It provided a comforting sound, especially at night when all was quiet.

I brought along my small harp. I played it for the three weeks during which Aunt Carmel was slowly dying and comatose. I played for her a selection of her favorite songs from the 1920's and 30's. These were from the Great American Songbook. Among them were songs by: Gershwin, Rodgers & Hart, Berlin, Cole Porter and others. I would play every evening for several hours in increments. Sometimes her eyelids would flicker. She died on July 5, 2008.

In the summer of 2009, Louie had an aortic aneurysm. He was airlifted to the hospital 30 minutes away from his Yucca Valley home. He died and was brought back twice on the operating table. After recovering here in Santa Monica, he returned to his home. That Christmas, he volunteered to deliver food to homebound people. Louie underwent spine surgery in 2010. He had been working in construction and was no longer able to. He had an old injury that he was procrastinating on treating. The surgery was not successful.

Me, Louie & Luanna (Christmas 2008)

On December, 8 2010 Louie became a grandfather. Jennifer gave birth to Sophia Claire. Luanna and I were so happy for Louie. He was youthful looking, belying his age. He was, at the same time, our "baby brother." Every time he called he would say "this is your baby brother." I started calling him that when he was already grown up. He sometimes acted as a big brother. He was always looking out for us and there when we needed him. Jennifer visited from Chanute, Kansas and Louie met Sophia in the spring of 2011. She was then three months old. Soon after, Julie gave birth to her son Athen Durand on May 14, 2011.

My cousin Dennis Hall was Aunt Carmel's youngest child. He died of a heart attack in October 2011. He was the head cameraman on the television series *Hawaii Five-0* since its inception in 1968. He was on location in New Orleans. He was working on the television series *Common Law*. He was 55 years old.

Our dear brother Louie was killed at the age of 67 in a tragic auto accident. It happened on December 22, 2011 in San Bernardino, California. He was coming home to Luanna and me for the holidays. He lived 130 miles from us. It seems like yesterday when we got the horrific news over the phone from the highway patrol. Louie made his Confirmation at age 12 and took the name Antonio, after our maternal Grandfather, Antonio DeLellis. It is ironic that they died in the same manner.

Louie's memorial Mass was held January 14, 2012 at Carondelet Center at the invitation of the nuns there. Father Bill (William Garcia), the chaplain at the center was very supportive when we lost Louie. The chapel was filled with over two hundred people including: large extended family, friends, Louie's classmates from elementary, high school, college and one of his teachers. Paul Alberghetti, his high school classmate, attended the service with his wife and son. Leonard DeMonte, another high school classmate died in 2009. He, Paul and Louie made up the three Italian boys hosted by Paul's sister, Anna Maria Alberghetti. Sister Grace Ann, his principal at Saint Bernadette Middle School, was there as well.

Three of the priests officiating at Louie's Funeral Mass were friends and classmates: Father Vincent Lopez of the Dominican Order was one of his teachers at Saint John Vianney High School, Monsignor David Sork was his classmate at Saint Bernadette Middle School and Father Allan Roberts was his classmate at Saint John Vianney High School. Father Roberts is now pastor at Saint Bernadette Church and School. Father William Wolfe, his classmate at Saint Bernadette's, was not able to join the other priests. He had commitments that Saturday at his own parish. He sent the most comforting card of condolence. Father John Roche was also one of the Celebrants.

The Sisters sang the Mass. Ellie Choate, a dear harpist friend of mine and Louie's played "My Buddy" for him. He was our "buddy." This was at the request of Luanna and me. Harpist friends who also attended were: Maria Casale, Liesl Erman, Carol Robbins and Buddy Halligan, Amy Shulman, Dorothy Victor and Amy Wilkins. If Ann Mason-Stockton had been alive, she would have been as devastated as we were. She sometimes invited Louie and his daughters for dinner when they were visiting us from Kansas.

Luanna and I then had a lovely catered Italian luncheon in the Sisters' huge dining room. Louie had come there with us many times for breakfast after attending Mass when he was in town. The

Sisters loved him. He was a great tease all of his life. They loved his playful side. Louie was a sweet man and baby brother.

I had a dream soon after losing Louie. There was nothing in it but the sound of guitars softly playing "Paradise" in a modified jazz version. "Paradise" is one of my favorite ballads of all time. It was composed by Nacio Herb Brown in 1931 with lyrics by Gordon Clifford. I don't think I ever told Louie it was special to me. I instantly knew it was a message from him. I can only interpret that dream as Louie telling me that he was all right and in Heaven. It is my only comfort.

On June 14, 2012 (Father's Day), Julie gave birth to Moses. In September of 2012, Jennifer gave birth to Brooke. Louie only saw Sophia Claire.

CHAPTER XIV

I gladly accepted the invitation to go with Holly and her family to North Dakota. This was a memorial celebration for Peg's 92nd birthday. It was a gift from Heaven. Peg's family is like our own to Luanna and me. Luanna chose to remain home and get some of her own projects done. She is interested in gardening and getting back to writing children's books. She attempted to get them published and got discouraged. I have seen these books. One is complete with illustrations. In my nonprofessional opinion, they are very good. I kept a journal of my North Dakota trip.

Thursday, May 24, 2012

We landed at Hector International Airport in Fargo, North Dakota. The large airport is beautiful and modern. We were met by Linda Grotberg and Carol Peterson. They were extremely nice people. They were responsible for organizing the entire three days and two evenings of events for Peg. After checking in at the Holiday Inn, Holly hosted a dinner for twenty-five people. It was at a restaurant called Doolittle's Woodfire Grill. It was a rustic place with huge fireplaces. The really delicious food was beautifully served. There were several members of the organizing committee and the press. Stacy Sullivan also attended. She is the singer who gave two tribute concerts for Peg on Friday and Saturday night.

Friday, May 25, 2012

We left the hotel early for the 1 ½ hour drive to Jamestown. Peg's two grandsons David and Michael Foster drove us all in two RVs (recreational vehicles). Our group included: Holly, her two young boys Carter and Keaton, Seth Berg (Peg's music promoter), David's wife Carol, Michael's son Teagan and me.

We arrived in Jamestown and were met by two other people

on the organizing committee. We then traveled to Nortonville to see the main street, old buildings and shops. One of them is now a gift shop and museum. It has two large windows with life-size pictures of Peg. Inside they have one of her gowns and some of her albums. Holly and I were interviewed there separately by a local television station. It was unexpected. They were affiliated with a national broadcasting company. Then we had lunch at Buffalo City Grille after scurrying around in Nortonville.

Afterward we went to the studio of WDAY Radio. This is where Peg sang as a teenager and later had her own show. This was before she left for California. WDAY is a beautiful facility now. The original station is where then owner Ken Kennedy gave Norma Deloris Egstrom the name Peggy Lee for broadcasting. Steve Urness, who works at the station, took my picture. He was extremely interested in my connection with Peg.

There is a museum there which was formerly an auto shop. It is large and houses an enormous skeleton of a dinosaur in perfect condition. The entire areas of: Jamestown, Nortonville and Wimbledon were underwater in prehistoric times.

We saw beautiful evergreen trees everywhere as we went through towns and highways. I never saw so many evergreen trees. The shades of green ranged from dark green to blue-green. It was like seeing infinite Christmas trees. There were no billboards anywhere.

In the afternoon we returned to Jamestown to see the following sites:

Park View Hospital – This is where Peg was born. It is on a charming residential street of old homes.

109 E Pittsburg Avenue South (now 109 7th Avenue SE) – This is the site of Peg's childhood home. It is near railroad tracks. It is now an empty lot after having burned down. It was an emotional experience. Peg suffered abuse there as a small child and later at the hands of her stepmother.

Saint John Lutheran Church – This is where Peg sang in the

choir. It was formerly known as German Lutheran Church. She made her Confirmation there at age 14 with her class in 1934. Peg was editor of the school paper at Wimbledon High School. She wrote a lengthy poem for her graduating class. I saw a faded framed copy of it in the church. There wasn't enough time to read it. We were told that her nickname in school was "Eggie" for Egstrom. I saw Confirmation photos of her sister, Marianne as well as those of her two older brothers, Leonard and Claire. Claire lived in California. Leonard was a hospital administrator in North Dakota. I met them both at Peg's home in the 50's.

Highland Home Cemetery – This is where Peg's father, Marvin Egstrom and infant sister, Gloria are buried. Peg's mother, Selma Anderson died when Peg was 4 years old. Selma is buried at First Lutheran Cemetery in South Dakota in her family plot.

After the tour we returned to the Inn. We had to get ready for Stacy Sullivan's tribute concert at 7:30 PM. Stacy performed at the Reiland Fine Arts Center at Jamestown College. Peg received her honorary Ph. D. in music there in 2000. Nicki accepted it on her behalf. Peg's portrait is on display there. The venue was filled for Stacy's tribute concert. There were four Japanese gentlemen who had come from Japan for the concert. I do not know their connection with Peg or what organization they represented, but it was announced. I know there has been a fan base in Japan since Peg's tour there in 1976.

Kate Stevenson is a professor at Jamestown College. She opened the concert and sang a short set of Peg's songs. She performed them in a really fine and unique style. When she sings Peg's up-tempo tunes she can really swing! This was not at all expected of a professor.

Stacy Sullivan created "A Tribute to Miss Peggy Lee" with Jon Weber on piano and Steve Doyle on bass. The entire program is a stroke of genius on the part of all three of them. Stacy has such respect for Peg's work. She treats Peg's repertoire of songs with an economy of her style. She sometimes uses only parts of songs or blends two or three together. One brilliant example is using the famous bass line of "Fever" at the beginning and end of "Cheek to Cheek." This version is sparing and terribly effective. Stacy was dressed tastefully in a conservative black gown. She is a tall and slim blonde. Her great love for Peg as a performer and person is evident in the way she talked throughout. I found a similar spirit in Stacy's personality as I had known in Peg's.

When I met Stacy at Holly's dinner the first night in Fargo, she treated me as though she knew me forever. This was because of *Sea Shells*. She asked me to autograph her copy of the original LP. She gave me a copy of her album *It's A Good Day – a Tribute to Miss Peggy Lee*. I asked her to autograph it for me and she wrote: For Stella, Angels on Your Pillow, With Love, Stacy Sullivan. There is an introduction to Stacy's album by Holly and a review by David Hajdu, music critic from *The New Republic*.

The concert was the debut of a never-before released song written by Peg and Paul Horner. The song is entitled "The Folks Back Home." Stacy's version is the first one recorded. The song is dedicated to the people of North Dakota. The concert lasted almost two hours with no intermission. We were mesmerized by the performance. Carter and Keaton, Peg's darling great-grandsons walked on stage. They presented Stacy with two gorgeous bouquets of roses, one yellow and one red. They looked so adorable in their navy blue suits, white shirts and ties.

There was then a lovely reception at the Reiland Center. The delicious food provided our group with dinner. There was no time before the concert after all of the sightseeing in Jamestown. There were so many nice people to talk to at the reception. I met a 98 year old woman who looked much younger. Her daughter went to school with Peg. We got back to the Inn well after midnight.

Saturday, May 26, 2012 (Peg's Birthday)

We left Jamestown at 9:30 AM for Wimbledon. It was a 45 minute drive. We were met at a junction leading into Wimbledon by the Wimbledon Volunteer Fire Department. The engine's red lights were flashing and sirens were blaring to escort the two RVs into Wimbledon. Carter, Keaton and Teagan had such fun riding with the firemen. We followed behind. Wimbledon is a small town with a population of just over 200.

We were led to an outdoor program with a drum and bugle corps for Memorial Day Weekend. The uniformed band played before the program of announcements. Mayor Roger Pickar was there for the opening of the Peggy Lee Exhibit at the Midland Continental Depot Museum. We were told about the planning and donations by several committees that made it possible. The site was erected in 1908 as the Midland Continental Railroad Depot. It began operations in 1913 and closed in 1970. It was intended to be part of a railroad extending from Canada to Texas.

Peg's father was passenger and freight agent there. Sometimes Peg worked there as a teenager substituting for him. She would sell tickets in a little office between school and working as a waitress at the Gladstone Hotel.

Most of the little depot building was replicated over a period of five years. This was done by local construction and renovation firms and other businesses in the county. The building is two stories with a kitchen and two bedrooms for the depot agent and family when needed. I saw one of the bedrooms where Peg slept. The furniture is duplicated. The kitchen had an original potbelly and wood burning stove with original cooking equipment. There is an oil painting by Peg of a nature scene. It is hung in one of the bedrooms.

The "Peggy Lee Room" is on the second floor. There are pictures and newspaper articles spanning Peg's career. They are chronologically placed on the walls. Displayed are pictures of David Barbour, the Benny Goodman Band with Peg and Nicki. There is a glass case with one of Peg's beaded gowns and silk shoes on a mannequin. There are two long drawers, each housing one of her gowns in them.

There is a listening nook with headphones to play Peg's music. The wall space in that section is covered with her album covers. Peg's voice was a gift from God. It was overwhelming seeing this shrine to her. It was like a tearful pilgrimage for me. I met journalist Steve Matthews. He said he was exceedingly glad to meet the harpist who created *Sea Shells* with Peg. He sought me out and was so kind. He spoke of his admiration for the album. He said he owned it for many years. I was grateful and thanked him.

Just next to the museum is an old barn that houses railroad equipment. It was long enough to accommodate a picnic for the entire Wimbledon population and guests. They served a hot lunch of roasted pork and shaved roast beef. The ladies served the meats in homemade buns with hot baked beans. For dessert there were cookies of all kinds and a huge homemade birthday cake. It was decorated in pink for Peg. They gave us huge help-yourself containers of Frosty Freeze ice cream. They were dreading rain that day. It mercifully did not "rain on Peg's parade." The rain didn't come until late that night. I felt sure she arranged that from Heaven and was having a good time watching everything.

We departed for Fargo at 2:00 PM. We saw Valley City, which is 43 minutes from Wimbledon. We visited the National Buffalo Museum. I saw buffalos grazing in the countryside. There were three white buffalos in the herd named White Cloud, Dakota Miracle and Dakota Legend. These animals are sacred to the indigenous Native American Tribes of the Northern Great Plains. There is a legend about The White Buffalo Calf Woman. The museum owns the world's largest steel statue of a buffalo. It is situated on the prairie. One of the committee members took a picture of all of us at the statue. It was freezing cold, as were all the days of the trip. That was overcome by the awesome sights we saw throughout.

Later that night was the second of Stacy Sullivan's tribute concerts. This one took place at a gorgeous venue called The Stage at Island Park at 7:00 PM. Holly or someone must have given my name to Steve Stark. He is a professor at Jamestown College. He is a humanities scholar, historian and illustrator who gave a pre-show presentation about Peg. Before his presentation, he had Peg's family and I take a bow. I was not expecting my name to be announced with them. The same thing happened at the outdoor program in Wimbledon.

Stacy repeated her concert to another full house. She had no affectation, no frills; she just stood there and sang as Peg did. Her hand movements recalled Peg's, even the look of her hands, with long graceful fingers. Her light banter was respectful and charming. In a light lilting voice she spoke of Peg and her family. I, like Holly, never thought I would enjoy anyone else who sang Peg's songs. We loved seeing the songs presented the way Stacy performed them. Stacy received a standing ovation. She was also given one at Friday's concert.

There was no time for dinner, but again there was a lovely reception. We had a banquet of: hot meatballs, hot artichoke dip, all kinds of crackers, chocolate covered strawberries, pastry, pink lemonade and wine. It was late getting back to the Inn after a wonderful evening.

Sunday, May 27, 2012

We had to leave at 7:00 AM. We had a flight departing at 8:55 AM for Minneapolis. After that we changed planes to get back to Los Angeles. It was worth every minute taking part in these wonderful activities. I got little sleep but had so much fun meeting many wonderful "downhome" people.

CHAPTER XV

I teach and coach still. I enjoy helping students and young professionals who need it in approaching or improving their concept of playing jazz harp. When I get to the harp for a lesson I don't teach by the hour. I do whatever it takes to be of real help. I have made many fine friends, young and old this way.

I think teachers can learn from their pupils. It's important to not be too formal and strict, and to teach with a degree of kindness. I am grateful I have arrived at this position myself. I practice and spend little time playing these days. I still hold workshops when invited. One was a Jazz Harp Workshop in Anaheim, California on July 8, 2009 at Salvi Harps.

It has been my privilege as a volunteer to play for Sunday Mass. I have done this since 1998 at Carondelet Center, the convent/residence of the Sisters of Saint Joseph of Carondelet. I play for the Sisters' funerals. The Order of Sisters of Saint Joseph of Carondelet educated all of us in grade school, as well as high school and Mount Saint Mary's College for Luanna. It's my small way of thanking them.

The harp I played in Peg's group lives in the chapel. It seems to like being there. The climate in there keeps the harp in tune. I almost never have to tune the entire 47 strings. That is a real blessing. This is unusual concerning the harp. I was inspired to call this harp "Peg." I hope she is pleased. It was the harp I played on *Sea Shells*.

When I first started playing for Sunday Mass, I would begin as the Sisters entered the chapel. One of them, in her 80's would do a little dance when I would play Cole Porter's "Begin The Beguine." I would see others swaying down the aisle. Some have told me that hearing those songs takes them back. They remember their younger years before entering the convent. One of them didn't like it much, so I had to stop playing from the Great American Songbook on Sundays. I now only play them for the Sisters' funerals as they enter the chapel for the Rosary Vigil. One of the Sisters has asked me to resume playing "the tunes" before Sunday Mass. The Sisters invite us to dinner on holidays. They tell Luanna and me "This is your home and you are always welcome. You can join us for breakfast, lunch and dinner any time." This is a great comfort.

The world is so full of love and coming together among human beings. Thankfully, Edgar and I met through emails regarding *Sea Shells* and his great interest in it in April of 2012. I have enjoyed bringing back my most wonderful association with Peg and the early years of our friendship. I'm sure Peg had something to do with our connecting.

It never entered my mind to write about my relationship to Peg as one of her musicians. I didn't consider myself to be of any importance. I pray to God to keep me well to finish this project and to give me a few more years. They say 82 years is not old anymore. I felt young throughout middle age. I still do most of the time. At times, I can be just as dumb as the teenager I once was.

On June 9, 2012 I went to a matinee of the great musical *Follies* with Luanna and Dorothy Victor. It was at the Los Angeles Music Center. It was really wonderful to see and hear it again. It lasted almost 3 ½ hours with intermission. It had been forty years since I played in it at the Shubert Theatre in Los Angeles. During its long run Katie Kirkpatrick, Lou Anne Neill and Dorothy Victor would also play in it for me.

Afterward Luanna, Dorothy and I went out to dinner. We hadn't dressed up and gone to any performance and dinner since Louie's death. It had been a while before that, too. The musical was a great means of concentration and release. Some of the music is emotional. Dorothy and I got teary-eyed. It was also emotional because Louie was not there to enjoy it. We miss him every day.

Luanna and I took a trip to Twin Falls, Idaho in June of 2012. We met up with Holly, her husband Dan and their boys Carter and

Keaton to visit Nicki. Nicki has been living there near Shoshone Falls. It was wonderful to see her again. I was glad to know she is still painting[1].

Holly and Dan drove us to Sun Valley for a sightseeing tour. We had always wanted to see Sun Valley. There is a historical lodge there that was the subject and locale of the film *Sun Valley Serenade*. It stars Sonja Henie, the ice skater who made movies in the 1930's and early 40's. Aunt Frances took me to see it when it was first released in 1941.

We also visited Dick Foster, who lives nearby with his girlfriend Angie Watson. Dick is Nicki's ex-husband and father of Holly, David and Michael.

Stacy Sullivan performed at Vitello's Jazz & Supper Club in Studio City on August 2, 2012. It was wonderful to see her Peg tribute concert again. Luanna saw it for the first time. Holly, her husband and their two little boys were there, as were Holly's brother David Foster, his wife Carol, Dick Foster and Angie Watson. They drove in from Nevada and Idaho, respectively. Holly's table had thirty people including Luanna and me. The small room was filled with at least one hundred people. It was sold out. Luanna was mesmerized, having had a personal friendship with Peg all through the years. It had such an impact on her, being familiar with the songs.

I decided to brace myself and go to the harp and "woodshed." This is a jazz term for holing oneself up for as long as one can stand and practice my "stuff." I prayed for all the Heavenly help I could get. I didn't think anything was happening until things came back slowly and then faster. I was unexpectedly hopeful that I would be able to give a reasonable performance for Edgar and Nick Vilches' visit here. I was "wrung out," as Luanna and I say when we are really exhausted from work around the house. We do the gardening that our gardener doesn't finish.

Ann Mason-Stockton once told me "You were put here for this." She was referring to my ability in playing jazz harp and

---

1   *(Nicki died on November 14, 2014 in Twin Falls, Idaho. This was just three days after her 71st birthday.)*

having a life dedicated to music. This is the life I've had instead of the one I had hoped for with marriage and children.

Jazz has its own rewards, spiritually, for me, and it is healing. It's been so long since I sat at my "ax" (another jazz term for one's instrument). I haven't used this vernacular since I was in Peg's groups. I had not played for some years except for the sacred music I play every Sunday Mass.

I had a TIA in 1998. It is a stroke of the smallest kind. Thankfully, I have been treated for it through medication ever since by a neurologist. He has told me I am doing fine. I don't have to see him until my regular biyearly appointments. I have noticed a change in my playing. It has also affected my memory. It doesn't seem to have affected me recalling things decades ago but the music is another thing.

I have not played in public since June of 2013. That was for The American Harp Society's Summer Institute. It was held at the Colburn Conservatory of Music in Los Angeles. Carol Robbins, Lori Andrews and I were invited to give a jazz harp workshop. It was a gratifying experience and a joy to be on the panel with them.

Luanna has been telling me for a long time to get back to practicing in the music room. I seem to have a block about disciplining myself. Everything is almost in my head as it should be for a jazz musician. It takes time to get it together in my fingers. For me there is a physical block to execute all of those "changes," as jazz harmonies are called. They are complex. That's why a lot of aspiring harpists shy away from them. They're much better at it now than I have observed in the past. It took a long time for these young people to even try to approach it. Why God gave me the grace to even begin to explore on my own I don't know.

Edgar and his friend Nick Vilches visited from Chicago in October of 2012. I played for them in the music room. I played: "Tea for Two," "The Maid with The Flaxen Hair," "Witchcraft," "I Remember You" and "Limehouse Blues." Those were the results of my "woodshedding." "Limehouse Blues" was in memory of my Uncle/Godfather Don for his birthday October 12th, which is the day I played for them. It was a challenge that I dearly needed. I thank God every day for not diminishing my sense of music. Nick was an enormous help to Edgar. He scanned a great amount of newspaper articles and photos of Peg during my tenure in her group and after.

Luanna and I went to Italy for Christmas of 2012 and New Year's. We spent the holidays with our cousins on Daddy's side of the family. They knew Louie from a visit he made as a young man in his twenties. Since learning of his death, they had been urging us to visit. We had not visited since 1979. This was the first break in our traditional tree trimming parties. We haven't had the heart to do it because Louie loved them so much. Our cousins were so welcoming through emails that had been going back and forth. Some live in Naples and Rome, but most are near Daddy's birthplace Apice. Apice is a one-hour drive from Naples.

Michael Amorosi was greatly devoted to Padre Pio, a Capuchin monk and priest. Padre Pio came from Pietrelcina, near the same area as Daddy. We visited the gardens and church there. I told Michael's sister Deborah of Michael's devotion. I sent her a book on Padre Pio from the gift shop there.

All aunts and uncles are now gone, all twelve of them. These include the ones by marriage, who were like actual blood relatives. I played for all of their funerals, having volunteered for this since 1972. The first time was for my Great-Uncle Tony. He was a WWI veteran. I then played the following year for my Grandmother. In the ensuing years there were many more for extended family and cherished friends. I want to do this and I will continue as long as I am able.

I love history, architecture, Egyptology, and biblical history. I am a movie buff. I especially enjoy those of the 1930's, 40's and some from the 50's. I love celebrating the birthdays of friends and family. I usually bake the cakes myself. I loved to bake since I was a child. I haven't baked much since losing Louie. He loved anything I baked for him throughout his life. He loved being with our friends for a special meal. He loved everything we cooked and especially desserts.

Our neighbors Dr. Richard and Catherine Corlin invited

Luanna and me to see Johnny Mathis perform. It was an event for Saint John's Health Center in Santa Monica, where Johnny was once a patient. He volunteered to give this concert for Saint John's. He had come to know the doctors and the nuns there. Dr. Corlin is head of the gastroenterology department.

I had told the Corlins in casual conversation that I played for several of Johnny's recording sessions in the 70's and 80's. Someone on the hospital board asked Johnny if he remembered me. He replied that he remembered me, my name and liked my playing.

Luanna had been ill with bronchitis since our return from Italy. Thanks to her feeling much better we did make it to the concert on February 23, 2013.

The Corlins picked us up for what would be an ever-so memorable evening. It was held at the Mullin Automotive Private Collection. Before the concert, we viewed a showroom of pre-World War I French touring automobiles. There was a magnificent array of perfectly restored cars from as early as 1900. It was an opulently-appointed building with enormous space for receptions, shows and dinners. Before our French bistro dinner Dr. Corlin introduced Luanna and me. He told the guests that I had played in the recording orchestra for several of Johnny's albums.

Johnny came on at 8:30 PM with his accompanying musicians. They were a marvelous quartet of exceptionally fine jazz musicians. He sang for over an hour. He sang many hit songs spanning his entire career. He was so gracious and relaxed in his presentation. He looked much younger than his 77 years and dressed stylishly casual.

We were seated ringside, practically under the stage. We were far enough for comfort and a great view. Johnny saw me at that close range and sang "Wonderful! Wonderful!" directly to Luanna and me. After he was finished singing, he said to the audience "That was personal." I couldn't believe it. He spoke to the audience and made them feel at home. The event raised $100,000 for Saint John's.

Dr. Richard Corlin, Me, Luanna & Catherine Corlin (2013)

After the concert there was a reception for Johnny. He appeared out of his suit. He was in casual leisure pants, shirt and regular tennis shoes. He patiently stood there while people came up to have pictures taken with him. Dr. Corlin called for me to come up with Luanna. Johnny and I hugged. I introduced him to Luanna. He seemed genuinely happy to see me after so many years, as I surely was to see him. He said "Hi, Sweetheart!" to Luanna.

It was the most wonderful happening for us after being holed up in our home for eight weeks with Luanna's illness. We were all dressed up. As I told the Corlins on the drive home, we felt like two Cinderellas wearing glass slippers. Dr. Corlin was the Prince and Catherine was our Fairy Godmother.

Notes

•

Only the recording sessions that Stella took part in are noted. Several Peggy Lee and other albums had additional recording dates.

The discography is not comprehensive. Stella has likely played on many more albums. The recordings included were confirmed through memory and research.

Acknowledgements from Stella

My gratitude and thanks to Edgar Amaya. Through his great love for Peggy Lee and her *Sea Shells* album this book was conceived. I would never have considered my part in the recording significant enough to merit Edgar seeking me out through a harp website. We began exchanging emails in May of 2012 and this book gradually took shape. It has created a journey of precious memories of my life as one of Peggy Lee's musicians and friends. "Peg," as I called her, was the "Big Sister" I never had.

Loving thanks to:

Nicholas Vilches, for scanning articles and pictures.
Nicki Foster, Peg's only daughter.
Holly Foster-Wells, Peg's granddaughter.
Laurie Allyn, a Peggy Lee fan and a truly fine singer of jazz and beautiful ballads in her own right.
Luanna Castellucci, my sister.

Stella Castellucci
October 5, 2013

Acknowledgements from Edgar

Balboa Press & Louise Hay – I am so glad to have this book associated with a great teacher.

Adriane Pontecorvo & Keelyn Walsh – Thanks for all of the encouragement and positivity in every step.

Iván Santiago-Mercado – Your website [http://www.peggyleediscography.com] was an immense help in piecing together dates. Your detail on recording sessions and release dates is amazing. You have done great research on all things Peggy Lee.

Robert Strom – Your book *Miss Peggy Lee A Career Chronicle* [McFarland & Company, Inc. 2005] would be a fine textbook for a class on Peggy Lee. It helped us to recall certain details.

Holly Foster-Wells – It was really the cherry on top to meet you and have your support on this.

Luanna Castellucci – You are one of the kindest and funniest people I know. Thanks for all of your support and letting me take so much of Stella's time as she worked with me.

Laurie Allyn – You have been with me ever since the first day I contacted you. You are a thoroughly beautiful person who beams with positivity and love. You have taken me to "Paradise."

Carrie Pierce – You got me on the right track with all of your great advice and experience. Thank you for answering so many of my questions.

Arvo Zylo – An amazingly creative and intelligent friend.

Lydia Lunch – You have been a supportive and loving friend for many years now. You inspire me in so many ways. You are a beautiful and honest person that I really look up to.

Nicholas Vilches – Thanks especially for all of your help during the first Santa Monica meeting. I am so glad you got to meet Stella and hear her play. You are an excellent friend and a major help in the final stages.

My grandmother: Elinor Bolke
My parents: Victoria Lopez, Fernando Amaya & Rosa Morgado
My siblings / best friends: Jazmin Tijerina & Eric Amaya

Antoni Maroto – Thanks for being very loving and patient. It means so much to have your support in everything that I do.

Stella Castellucci:

You are a remarkable human being. You possess a warm, honest and pure heart. Since meeting you, I have undergone many changes and healing processes. I went into this wanting to "dive deep" and find out all I could about *Sea Shells*. You gave me that and so much more. Seeing you before my very eyes playing "The Maid with The Flaxen Hair" (and others) was a "religious experience." It overwhelmed me in the best possible way. You are inherently a big sister to many. The same way Peggy Lee was for you. Thank you for your trust in me to do this with you. It is the greatest gift. You have taught me so much.

Edgar Amaya
November 27, 2013

Session Work Discography

1947 Louis Castellucci Military Band / Here Comes The Band!
"Stars and Stripes Forever," "French National Defile March,"
"Washington Post March," "Parade of The Wooden Soldiers,"
"Semper Fidelis," "El Capitan," "Anchors Aweigh," "Lights
Out"

1950 Louis Castellucci & The Capitol Symphonic Band / A
Festival of Symphonic Band Music
"Scenes from The Sierras," "Sleigh Ride," "Lohengrin:
Introduction to Act 3," "The Syncopated Clock," "Jesu, Joy of
Man's Desiring," "Pavanne," "Sarabande," "Trumpet Tune,"
"Funiculi Funicula "

1952 Charlie Chaplin / Limelight (included on 2003 Two-Disc
Special Edition DVD)

1953 Bernard Herrmann / Beneath the 12-Mile Reef
Peggy Lee / Baubles, Bangles and Beads / Love You So
(Single)
Peggy Lee / Ring Those Christmas Bells / It's Christmas
Time Again (Single)
Peggy Lee / Apples, Peaches and Cherries / The Night
Holds No Fear (For The Lover) (Single)

1954 Peggy Lee / Songs in An Intimate Style
Peggy Lee / It Must Be So (Single)
Paul J. Smith / 20,000 Leagues Under The Sea

1956 Peggy Lee / Black Coffee with Peggy Lee

1957 Peggy Lee / Dream Street
Peggy Lee / The Man I Love

Walter Gross / Plays His Own Great Songs
Laurie Allyn / Paradise (unreleased until 2004)
Recorded: Hollywood, CA, October 2-5, 1957
Ella Fitzgerald & Louis Armstrong / Porgy & Bess
Recorded: Capitol Tower, Hollywood, August 18 & 19, 1957
Mel Tormé / Mel Tormé's California Suite
Recorded: Radio Recorders, Hollywood, CA, March 11 & 13,
1957

1958 **Peggy Lee** / Sea Shells (Recorded in 1955)
Peggy Lee / Jump for Joy
Mel Tormé / Prelude to a Kiss
Recorded: Radio Recorders, Hollywood, CA, November
1957
Orrin Tucker / The New Sounds of Orrin Tucker
Sonny James / Honey!

1959 **Peggy Lee** / It Ain't Necessarily So / Swing Low, Sweet
Chariot (Single)
Dean Martin / Sleep Warm
Recorded: Capitol Tower, Hollywood, October 14, 1958
Alfred Newman / The Diary of Anne Frank

1960 **Peggy Lee** / Merry Christmas From Peggy Lee - Jingle Bells
(I Like A Sleighride) / Christmas Carousel (Single)
Peggy Lee / Pretty Eyes
Peggy Lee / Christmas Carousel

1962 **Frances Faye** / Swinging All the Way with Frances Faye
Recorded: Radio Recorders, Hollywood, November 24,
1961

1963 **George McCurn** / I'm Just A Country Boy / In My Little
Corner Of The World (Single)

1965 **Ray Conniff and His Orchestra & Chorus** / Friendly
Persuasion
Ray Charles / Without A Song (Single)

1966 **Maurice Jarre** / Grand Prix
Jack Jones / All or Nothing At All (Single)

1967 **Tina Mason** / Is Something Wonderful!
Frederick Loewe / Camelot

1968 **The Sugar Shoppe** / The Sugar Shoppe

1969 **Steve John Kalinich** / A World of Peace Must Come
(unreleased until 2008)
Carpenters / Ticket To Ride (Single)

1970 **Jackson 5** / ABC
Jackson 5 / Third Album

1972 **Michael Jackson** / Ben
The Osmonds / Crazy Horses (Single)
Barbra Streisand / Live Concert at The Forum
Recorded: April 5, 1972

1973 **Lamont Dozier** / Out Here on My Own
Barry White / I'm Gonna Love You Just a Little More Baby
(Single)
Barry White / Never, Never Gonna Give Ya Up (Single)
Diana Ross & Marvin Gaye / Diana & Marvin

1974 **Barry White** / Can't Get Enough
Barry White Featuring The Love Unlimited Orchestra /
Rhapsody in White

1975 **Waters** / Waters
Recorded: Music Recorders, Los Angeles, October 22-23,
1974
Earth, Wind & Fire / That's The Way of The World
Barry White / Let The Music Play (Single)

1976 **Barry White** / Don't Make Me Wait Too Long (Single)
Jimmy Jackson / Rollin' Dice
"Something's Burning," "You Say You Love Me More" &
"Romeo and Juliet"
Frankie Crocker's Heart and Soul Orchestra / Presents
The Disco Suite Symphony No. 1 in Rhythm and Excellence
Snuff Garrett's Texas Opera Company / Classical Country
Seals & Crofts / Get Closer (Single)

1977 **João Gilberto** / Amoroso
José Feliciano / Angela
"As Long As I Have You"
Maxi Anderson / Maxi
Recorded: Barnum Studios, L.A. & ABC Recording Studios,
L.A., February 16-17, 1977
Helen Reddy / Ear Candy
Eloise Laws / Eloise

1978 **Lee Oskar** / Before The Rain
Ted Gärdestad / Blue Virgin Isles
Cheryl Lynn / Cheryl Lynn
Toto / Toto
John Williams / Jaws 2

1980 **Donna Washington** / For The Sake Of Love
Earl Klugh / Dream Come True

1981 **Earl Klugh** / Crazy For You
João Gilberto / Brasil

1982 **José Feliciano** / Escenas De Amor
Maynard Ferguson / Hollywood
"Touch and Go"

1983 **José Feliciano** / Me Enamore
Earl Klugh / Low Ride

1985 **Steve Arrington** / Dancin' In The Key of Life
"Willie Mae"

2000 **Abby Travis** / Cutthroat Standards & Black Pop
"Everything's Wonderful"

2006 **Nick Lemieux** / Another Angel Watching

2007 **Jan A.P. Kaczmarek** / Evening [Music From and Inspired
By the Motion Picture]

2010 **Jimmy Haslip featuring Joe Vannelli** / Nightfall
"Nightfall"

UNK   Steve Shakarian / The Wonder of It All

COMPILATIONS
(Exact Details Unknown)

Ann-Margret / 1961-1966 (2004)
The Beach Boys / Made in California (2013)
Bill Withers / Lean on Me: The Best of Bill Withers (1994)
Commodores / Anthology (1995)
Dave Mason / Ultimate Collection (1999)
Diana Ross / Forever Diana Musical Memoirs (1993)
Duane Eddy / Deep in The Heart of Twangsville The Complete
        RCA Victor Recordings - 1962-1964 (1999)
Eddie Kendricks / The Best of Eddie Kendricks: 20th Century
        Masters: Millennium Collection (2000)
Friends of Distinction / The Best of Friends of Distinction (1996)
Jack Jones / Greatest Hits (1995)
Johnny Mathis/ 16 Most Requested Songs (1990) / The Christmas
        Music of Johnny Mathis: A Personal Collection (1993)
Lionel Richie / The Definitive Collection (2003)
Marvin Gaye / Every Motown Hit of Marvin Gaye (1983)
Minnie Ripperton / Free Soul - The Classics of Minnie Riperton
        (1999)
Nat King Cole / Stardust: The Complete Capitol Recordings
        1955-1959 (2006)
Phil Spector / Back to Mono 1958-1969 (1991)
Recorded: RCA Victor Studio 1, Hollywood, August 13, 1963 &
        October 23-24, 1963
Rosemary Clooney / Many a Wonderful Moment (2000)
Sonny James / Young Love: The Complete Recordings 1952-62
        (2002)
Various / Now That's What I Call Christmas! Vol. 3 (2006)

Stella Castellucci Discography

1997 Lights & Shadows Vol. I

1998 Lights & Shadows Vol. II
"A Little Swing, a Little Latin and Other Things"

2002 Lights & Shadows Vol. III
For Lovers Everywhere... Part I

2003 Lights & Shadows Vol. IV
For Lovers Everywhere... Part II

Stella Castellucci Bibliography

Rhythm for Harp (with Verlye Mills)
Hollywood, CA: Vignette Production Music, 1973.
[out of print]

Available through:
http://www.us.harp.com

An Approach to Jazz and Popular Music for Harp
Los Angeles, CA: Miranda Publications, 1983. 363 Pages

Available through:
Lyon & Healy West
1037 E South Temple
Salt Lake City, UT 84102
USA
http://www.lyonhealy.com/lhwest.htm

Bibliography

CHAPTER I
"Castellucci's Italians" – *University Misourian*, August 16, 1915
"Omero Castellucci, the peerless bandmaster"–*The Daily Missourian*, July 18, 1917
"There's a bracing exhilaration" – *Adair County News*, July 17 & 24, 1918
"Chautauqua week brings splendid" – *The Evening Herald*, May 22 & 24, 1919
"Castellucci and his musicians" – *Woodland Daily Democrat*, May 14, 1919

CHAPTER III
"His natural sense of perfect pitch" – *The Catalina Islander*, September 18, 1941
"It was the flashback" – *Home of The Brave (Profiles of American Veterans)*, American Veteran's Center, 2010

CHAPTER VI
"Peggy Lee is probably the only" – *Los Angeles Examiner*, (date unknown)
"[I sculpt] Mostly hands" – Hickey, *The American Weekly*, July 3, 1960 p. 10
"One close friend believes" – Baskette, *Redbook*, April 1955
"Peggy Lee is so ill she had to skip a night" – Parsons, *The Milwaukee Sentinel*, June 27, 1953
"Last year I planned six months ahead" – Baskette, *Redbook*, April 1955
"Peggy Lee who now carries" – Downbeat, August, 12, 1953
"Miss Lee possesses a smooth" – *Hollywood Bowl Magazine*, September 1953
"When I recorded 'Baubles'" – Gleason, *San Francisco Chronicle*, June 13, 1954
"Peggy Lee, in her Ciro's" – Connolly, *The Hollywood Reporter*,

March 24, 1954

"She [Peg] was taking" – Newton, *San Francisco Examiner*, June 9, 1954

"TV show working title" – Newton, *San Francisco Examiner*, June 9, 1954

"She currently is dickering" – Gleason, *Downbeat*, July 14, 1954

"There's something wrong here" – Leonard Feather, *Laughter From The Hip*, 1963

CHAPTER VII

"She looked around the small apartment" – Whitcomb, *Cosmopolitan*, February 1955 p. 57

"Of all the stringed instruments" – Lee, Peggy. "About the Harp" on back cover, Peggy Lee: *Sea Shells*. Decca DL8591, 1958. LP Recording.

"Besides countless popular" – Baskette, *Redbook*, April 1955

"They were chosen more" – Lee, Peggy. "About the Selections" on back cover, Peggy Lee: *Sea Shells*. Decca DL8591, 1958. LP Recording.

"Gene DiNovi... who is" – Lee, Peggy. "About the Artists" on back cover, Peggy Lee: *Sea Shells*. Decca DL8591, 1958. LP Recording.

"A neighbor in their" – Baskette, *Redbook*, April 1955

"I was interested in older people" – Gould, *New York Times*, June 19, 1955

"They are Chinese love poems" – Lee, Peggy. "About the Chinese poems" on back cover, Peggy Lee: *Sea Shells*. Decca DL8591, 1958. LP Recording.

"Peggy Lee, she with the celestial" – Wong, *The Chinese World*, June 11, 1955

"I like the imaginative trend that" – Lee, *Los Angeles Examiner*, April 4, 1954

"A quality set of recordings" – *Billboard*, May 19, 1958

CHAPTER VIII

"I modeled that part on" – Hickey, *The American Weekly*, July 3, 1960 p. 10

"Whenever I go to do anything" – Smith, *Los Angeles Times*, August 16, 1959

"Peg Lee's new record album" – Kennedy, *Los Angeles Evening Herald Express*, August 12, 1953

"Peggy's concern with important details" – Tynan, *Downbeat*, March 21, 1957 p. 13

"In recent years, she reflected" – Tynan, *Downbeat*, March 21, 1957 p. 13

"In rehearsal, Peggy has" – Tynan, *Downbeat*, March 21, 1957 p. 13

CHAPTER IX

"Miss Lee does her cogitating" – Mangano, *McCall's*, February 1958

"Ciro's was packed elbow" – *Los Angeles Examiner*, August 1960

"Exciting Peggy Lee, Capitol" – Wright, *Los Angeles Herald & Express*, August 2, 1960

CHAPTER X

"Warner is actually a walking" – *Star News*, June 27, 1964

"On busy Saturday nights" – *Valley News*, September 25, 1964

"Those who know her best" – Berges, *The Los Angeles Times Home Magazine*, October 19, 1975

CHAPTER XI

"The weekend's New York concert" – Elwood, *San Francisco Examiner*, June 7, 1995

CHAPTER XII

"The Castle Light Records release" – Kelly, *The Harp Column*, November / December 1997

"Castellucci voices chords better" – Kelly, *The Harp Column*, January / February 1999

CHAPTER XIII

"I am guided in life by" – Doye, *Beverly Hills [213]*, May 4, 1994

About The Authors

Edgar Amaya & Stella Castellucci (2013)

Stella Castellucci reached the pinnacle of her profession as a jazz harpist and composer through multiple avenues. She started in radio as a staff musician for the American Broadcasting Company in Hollywood when she was nineteen. After two years at ABC, she entered an eight-year association with famed singer Peggy Lee. She is co-author, with the late Verlye Mills, of *Rhythm for Harp*

(1973). Since 1974, her deep interest in conducting workshops in jazz harp has added a new dimension to her career. She wrote *An Approach to Jazz and Popular Music for Harp* in 1983. She was an invited soloist at the 1987 World Harp Congress in Vienna and at the American Harp Society conferences of 1985 in Columbus, Ohio and 2000 in Cincinnati, Ohio. For her arrangements of standard and contemporary songs and ballads, Miss Castellucci has been lauded by harpists everywhere. Many can be heard on her CDs *Lights & Shadows*. She lives in Santa Monica, California.

Edgar Amaya has always surrounded himself with words and music. His articles have appeared in: *Lumpen, Meefers, Roctober* and *Wet Noise*. He has previously published *Greatest Improvement in Dance* (2009), a collection of music interviews and reviews. His poetry chapbooks include: *Intro Extro Internal: The Manikin's Manifesto* (2001), *Threat II: Anonymous* (2004) and *Doom EmotIIlon* (2005). He is part of the audio/visual duo EaViL. He also writes, performs and DJs as RODENTAL. He lives in Barcelona.

CPSIA information can be obtained
at www.ICGtesting.com
Printed in the USA
FSOW01n0007260516
20818FS

MEMORIAL LITURGY
for
ROSE M. WOJCIECHOWSKI
(April 15, 1928 - January 16, 2017)

In Loving Memory

Plant me a garden under the sun
Plant me a garden before day is done.
Fill it with roses, sweet will they grow.
Fill it with lilies, pure as the snow.

Plant me a garden to nourish my soul.
Plant me a garden, make me feel whole.
Fill it with hope, surround it with grace.
Fill it with faith, this sanctified place.

Plant me a garden, nourished from above.
Plant me a garden, and sow it with love.

Presiding Priest	Fr. Steven Bauer (Nephew)
	Msgr. Francis X. Blood
	Msgr. John J. Leykam

Entrance Rite

Entrance Song	You Are Mine
First Reading	Sister Connie Bauer O.P.
Responsorial	Shepard Me O God
Second Reading	Sister Celine Birk, A.S.C.
Alleluia	Celtic
Gospel	
Homily	
Petitions	Sheila Hoffman
Preparation of Gifts	I have Loved You
Offertory Gifts	Hayley Wojciechowski
	Clare Wojciechowski
	Shawnee Wojciechowski
Communion Song	No Greater Love
	Beautiful Savior
	You Raised Me Up
Eulogy	Tammy Wojciechowski
	David Wojciechowski

Song of Commendation	Come to Her Aid
Recessional	Amazing Grace #442

Music and Vocals	Dan & Carol Bauer
	Mike Bauer
Pall Bearers	Paul Wojciechowski
	Adam Wojciechowski
	Nicholas Wojciechowski
	Mike Hoffman
	Erik Helms
	Matt Tiefenbrunn

Plant Me A Garden by Janet Collins
A Mother's Journey author unknown

Luncheon will be held at Holy Trinity parish gym after
burial (approx. 1:00 pm).

A Mother's Journey

A young mother set her foot on the path of life. "Is this the long way?" she asked. And the guide said, "Yes, and the way is hard. And you will be old before you reach the end of it. But the end will be better than the beginning." But the young mother was happy, and she would not believe that anything could be better than these years. So, she played with her children, she fed them and bathed them, taught them how to tie their shoes, ride a bike, reminded them to feed the dog, do their homework and brush their teeth. The sun shone on them, and the young Mother cried, "nothing will ever be lovelier than this." Then the nights came, and the storms, and the path was sometimes dark, the children shook with fear and cold, and the mother drew them close and covered them with her arms, and the children said," Mother, we are not afraid, for you are near, and no harm can come." The morning came, and there was a hill ahead, and the children climbed and grew weary, and the mother was weary. But, at all times, she said to the children, "A little patience and we are there." So, the children climbed, and as they climbed they learned to weather the storms. And with this, she gave them strength to face the world. Year after year, she showed them compassion, understanding, hope, but most of all ...*unconditional* love. And when they reached the top they said, "Mother, we would not have done it without you." The days went on, and the weeks and the months and the years, and the mother grew old and she became little and bent. But her children were tall and strong, and walked with courage. The mother when she lay down at night, looked up at the stars and said, "This is a better day than the last, for my children have learned so much and are now passing these traits on to their children."
When the way became rough for her, they lifted her, and gave her strength, just as she had given them hers. One day they came to a hill, and beyond the hill, they could see a shining road and golden gates flung wide open. The Mother said, "I have reached the end of my journey. And now I know the end is better than the beginning, for my children can walk with dignity and pride, with their heads held high, and so can their children after them." And the children said, "You will always walk with us, Mother, even when you have gone through the gates." They stood and watched her as she went on alone, and the gates closed after her. And they said, "We cannot see her, but she is with us still. A Mother like ours is more than a memory. She is a living presence." Your Mother is always with you. She's the whisper of the leaves as you walk down the street, she's the smell of certain foods you remember, flowers you pick and perfume that she wore, she's the cool hand on your brow when you're not feeling well, she's your breath in the air on a cold winter's day. She is the sound of the rain that lulls you to sleep, and the colors of a rainbow, she is Christmas morning. Your Mother lives inside your laughter. And she's crystallized in every tear drop. A Mother shows every emotion.....happiness, sadness, fear, jealousy, love, hate, anger, helplessness, excitement, joy, sorrow and all the while, hoping and praying you will only know the good feelings in life. She's the place you came from, your first home, and she's the map you follow with every step you take. She's your first love, your first friend, even your first enemy, but nothing on earth can separate you.
Not time, not space.........not even death!